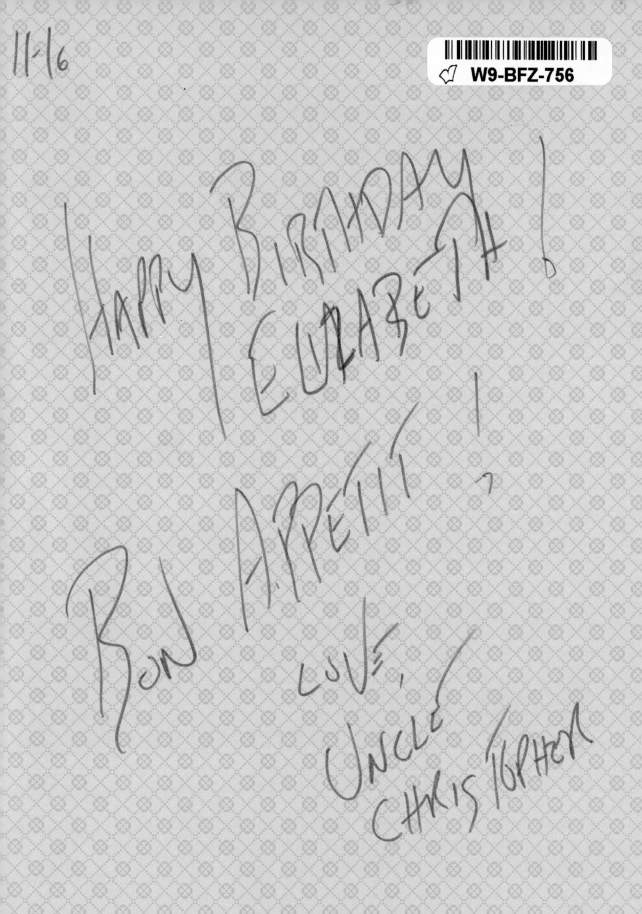

Happy Birthday Elizabeth!

Bon Appetit!

Love,
Uncle
Christopher

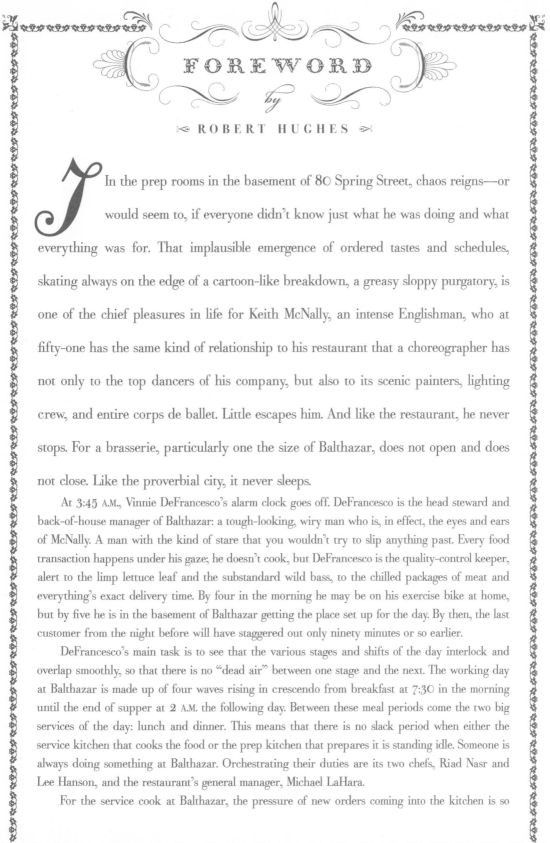

FOREWORD

by

ROBERT HUGHES

In the prep rooms in the basement of 80 Spring Street, chaos reigns—or would seem to, if everyone didn't know just what he was doing and what everything was for. That implausible emergence of ordered tastes and schedules, skating always on the edge of a cartoon-like breakdown, a greasy sloppy purgatory, is one of the chief pleasures in life for Keith McNally, an intense Englishman, who at fifty-one has the same kind of relationship to his restaurant that a choreographer has not only to the top dancers of his company, but also to its scenic painters, lighting crew, and entire corps de ballet. Little escapes him. And like the restaurant, he never stops. For a brasserie, particularly one the size of Balthazar, does not open and does not close. Like the proverbial city, it never sleeps.

At 3:45 A.M., Vinnie DeFrancesco's alarm clock goes off. DeFrancesco is the head steward and back-of-house manager of Balthazar: a tough-looking, wiry man who is, in effect, the eyes and ears of McNally. A man with the kind of stare that you wouldn't try to slip anything past. Every food transaction happens under his gaze; he doesn't cook, but DeFrancesco is the quality-control keeper, alert to the limp lettuce leaf and the substandard wild bass, to the chilled packages of meat and everything's exact delivery time. By four in the morning he may be on his exercise bike at home, but by five he is in the basement of Balthazar getting the place set up for the day. By then, the last customer from the night before will have staggered out only ninety minutes or so earlier.

DeFrancesco's main task is to see that the various stages and shifts of the day interlock and overlap smoothly, so that there is no "dead air" between one stage and the next. The working day at Balthazar is made up of four waves rising in crescendo from breakfast at 7:30 in the morning until the end of supper at 2 A.M. the following day. Between these meal periods come the two big services of the day: lunch and dinner. This means that there is no slack period when either the service kitchen that cooks the food or the prep kitchen that prepares it is standing idle. Someone is always doing something at Balthazar. Orchestrating their duties are its two chefs, Riad Nasr and Lee Hanson, and the restaurant's general manager, Michael LaHara.

For the service cook at Balthazar, the pressure of new orders coming into the kitchen is so great that a mistake in thoroughly setting up his station can cost him his job. "During the shift, there's such a colossal sense of urgency," says McNally, "that whether you're a cook, a waiter, or a bartender you *have* to be set up. You have to have your tools and a backup of tools in place and the *same* place at all times. Otherwise you sink and never recover." The kitchen staff are like a culinary version of the engineers and maintenance staff in the pit during an auto race: fumble, delay, lose a wrench, and you won't catch up.

It is the job of the floor staff, from the busboys to the maître d'hotel, to dissimulate the pressure, smooth it over, make it seem as if it weren't there. Nobody wants to eat in a pressure cooker, yet that is what any restaurant of this size would seem to be if you took the lid off for a moment, and the walls between the dining room and the service kitchen were made transparent. So out on the floor it's all politeness, smiles, and yes-sir-no-sir, while backstage it's Jesus, where is it, get that fucking stuff over here, and where's the goddamn morels?

It's six A.M. in downtown Manhattan. SoHo is quite dead except for a delivery truck making its way to the loading dock of Balthazar, where chefs Riad Nasr and Lee Hanson are now checking in. Some of their coworkers have been in the preparation kitchen for an hour or more already. One of them is Cesar, who is in the basement preparing the *plat du jour* for Monday, a week from today. It will be *poitrine de veau*, or breast of veal. Ninety-one pounds of the cut have been ordered by the chefs, weighed in by DeFrancesco, and then hand-trucked into the prep kitchen by Cesar. Here, those five whole breasts will be seared to hold in their juices and then braised.

The tool for doing this is a rectangular braiser with a hinged lid, about 8 inches deep by 20 long and 30 wide. A cup of olive oil goes into it, followed by the chunks of veal breast, lightly floured, which brown and sizzle impressively. This machine works at a higher temperature than you will ever get in your kitchen fry pan. The whole receptacle of the fryer is hinged so that it can tip forward to pour off the rendered fat—not that there is much, the meat being rather lean veal.

The braising liquid, along with a bright orange mirepoix dominated by carrots, is added when the chunks of breast are nice and brown. The liquid is an indecently rich brown stock, made by simmering a mass of chicken parts, cut-up bones, and root vegetables previously fried caramel brown, plus mushroom parings and the like. It's prepared in the soup broiler to the left of the fryer, a massive device made by a company called Groen, which can hold 80 gallons at one filling. You half expect the skull of a restaurant critic who has incurred the displeasure of Hanson and Nasr to bob briefly and reproachfully to the surface, greasily turn, and then sink. But no such thing happens. Would anyone find the *corpus delicti* if it did? Don't bet on it.

The veal breast comes out tender but chewy, not stringy exactly, but with a bite to it, a texture enlivened by the sweetness of the carrots. It will carve neatly.

A young guy is cutting up onions, *chunka, chunka-chunk,* the ten-inch knife reducing them to a mass of small, even julienne. Extractor fans roar in the ceiling.

The day's mushrooms are in. One mushroom cutter deals with waxed boxes of cepes, which grow wild in American woods; the restaurant uses about 40 pounds of them a day. Another slicer attacks the Japanese shiitakes, three boxes a day, say 27 pounds. They come in clean, no need for scrubbing. Their canopies are sliced and their stems saved to throw in the stock. Plus, there's box after box of cultivated button mushrooms.

Another worker preps the garlic, whacking the heads with a short wooden truncheon to split the skins, dumping the separated cloves to soak in a plastic tub of water so that the skins will slip off. Thirty pounds of garlic are used every week. A generation ago, no New York restaurant would have used that much in two months. Tastes change; most of us would have found the restaurant dishes of our fathers uninterestingly bland, because they had to be geared to an "average" palate that found strong savors too aggressively tinged with foreignness. Today, garlic is fundamental to the earthy palette of brasserie food.

But not all fruits of the earth are suitable for brasserie cooking these days. Forget about truffles, white or black: they are so expensive as to be commercially untouchable. *Funghi porcini*, those slightly obscene-looking forest mushrooms with the dark brown caps and swollen waists, the same: they are in short supply this autumn, but they may multiply out of sight next year. Or not. There is no predicting. Too unreliable.

The french fries are being readied. You cannot have a brasserie without french fries. Probably if it weren't for brasseries they wouldn't even be called french fries. "The fries are crucial," says Riad Nasr. "In a brasserie you can have really fantastic food, but if the fries are limp or greasy or burned, people will remember it." No over-mechanization here: there is a doodad on the wall with a cutting grid set within it, and the peeled potato goes into that like an egg into an egg slicer. One downward swipe with the handle, and the cut fries, separated, fall into a tub of water for a soak that dissolves out some of their starch.

Every day the kitchen does fifteen 50-pound cases of spuds. They are all peeled, incredible as it seems at first, by hand, by a single man with a slotted swivel-knife. This is Cepe Gomez, an immigrant from the Dominican Republic. "He has amazing concentration," says Riad with a certain awed respect. "He can do it for hours at a stretch and never lose intensity." The idea of "intensity" associated with potato peeling seems like a stretch, but on reflection one realizes that it applies—as any Zen adept could tell you.

Fifteen cases of Idaho russets cook out 750 pounds of fries a day, somewhat more than 2 tons a week. (Then there is a considerable bulk of Yukon Gold potatoes, used not for fries but for mash—the topping of one of the establishment's more popular dishes, the duck shepherd's pie.) Brasserie eaters don't like it if the place is stingy with the fries. Leaving aside the astronomical quantities of precooked and reheated fries produced by the likes of McDonald's, which are not brasserie fries in any authentic sense (and of course do not even taste like an echo of them), this is the largest production of hand-cut fries in any serious restaurant in America. Though procedures back in the "classical" days of the French brasserie—the 1890s, say—called for rendered beef lard as the cooking medium, Balthazar prefers peanut oil (at 400°F.) to fry them: a bland, neutral medium that does not burn the potatoes, or catch fire, as easily as animal fat.

The day's fish arrive at the loading bay, gleaming and speckled with crushed ice, but never frozen. The time is long past when the restaurant's fish cook went down to Fulton Street and chose the fish himself, peering at the eyes for telltale sunkenness, checking the gills for the brown tinge that betrays a stale fish. The restaurant has suppliers that DeFrancesco trusts —here, as elsewhere in Balthazar, all decisions about the quality of the ingredients devolve on DeFrancesco at the outset, and then on Nasr and Hanson. It's up to these wholesalers to make sure the fish are bright, clear, and fresh from the water. Otherwise the relationship breaks down.

You can't deceive a professional cook with even slightly substandard seafood. Professional cooks have eyes like eagles or, rather, ospreys. It takes fresh wild salmon, flounder, striped bass, gray or sea bass, and the skate wings that, lightly floured and then sautéed with brown butter, capers, and a mere gout of vinegar, make one of the place's best brasserie dishes, the *raie au beurre noir*. (Skate is a particularly good brasserie fish because it keeps: some cooks say it eats better two days dead than absolutely fresh.) Balthazar uses a lot of smallish lobsters: while all the finfish are dead before they are cooked, *Palinurus vulgaris* is useless if it dies before cooking time. Properly handled, it will stay alive out of water far longer than any finfish.

Balthazar will not touch bluefish, which are good only when just taken from the sea, and start to go mushy in one day; any bluefish in the market is suspect, and even dockside you would want to know how long the fishing boat has been out.

Then there is the meat. It is a paradox that some of the most delicious cuts of beef leave America more or less automatically, heading for where the market is. An example is hanger steak, a robust and flavorsome meat that, for inherited cultural reasons, Americans never seem to want. Almost all of it ends up in Japan, whose gastronomes do want it. But Americans are reluctant to order cuts of meat in a restaurant that they aren't familiar with from the supermarket, and the waiter who tries to explain to the diner exactly at hanger steak is is likely to be met with incomprehension. So you will not find it in Balthazar.

"American supermarkets don't butcher meat properly, in the real sense," says Riad Nasr. "They just saw up a cow," and take the least possible trouble to dissect individual cuts. "You get all sorts of muscles in there, whereas a French butcher cuts along the lines of the fiber." The nomenclature is different, and some French names correspond to no American cut. Every muscle group has its own characteristics. "This is good for tenderloin," he says, "this is perfect for braising, this for boiling, and this tiny little top muscle is beautifully tender on its own, so I'll save it right there."

The chefs at Balthazar break down most of their meat in the kitchens, from large anatomical units supplied by a wholesale butcher. The steak frites, for instance, is cut from a piece known as the top butt. A 15-pound piece yields about 7 usable pounds of steak; the rest, with red wine and shallots and the usual traditional ingredients, becomes meat stock. The quality of a brasserie depends on, among other crucial things, the quality of its meat and seafood stocks, those liquid essences that have to be made in house (we're not talking about Coca-Cola here) and are absolutely essential to the style of the chefs and the character of their food.

Vacant except for its skeleton floor staff, not a customer in sight yet, the cavernous dining room of Balthazar is reminiscent of a stage set not yet occupied by its actors. This is fitting and deliberate: Keith McNally set it up that way, building it from scratch in order to give the illusion that everything is where it always has been: no-décor décor. Originally it was just a big room with a high ceiling, like many others in SoHo. McNally loves rooms like that—rather grimy, or at least dusty, empty canvases that he will endow with the traces of memories that don't actually exist.

It's hard not to grasp that McNally sees the task of making a restaurant, finishing it down to the last detail, as a utopian enterprise, more than a mere stage setting, yet having some of the qualities of theater. He will take, as at Balthazar, a large neutral space with no particular character of its own and laboriously endow it not with Louis-something splendor, but with the worn, browned, chipped, and tobacco-fugged look of a place that has been there for ages.

Balthazar has enormous mirrors in wooden frames with arched tops: the biggest of them must be 15 feet wide. The mirrors look as though they were made about a mile from where Charles de Gaulle was born. Not so. Though old, they all came from within a five-hour radius of Manhattan; Keith is quite categorical about this, having done the driving himself. He bought scores of small beat-up mirrors, already foxed, silver-speckled, fogged, and aged. Their collective weight was imposing, dreadnought-like. Workmen then constructed an iron chassis to take the weight, and the mirrors were screwed to quarter-inch plywood, which in turn was bolted to the chassis, with lead strips—something like the framing of a stained-glass window—in the joints. Then they were assembled and cut together, a shifting collage of dimly reflective surfaces, like the background of a Braque café still life that is too big to ever have existed. The frames, however, are new.

These mirrors ended up completely obscuring large windows that had already been there for years, on the Crosby Street side of the dining room. Some of McNally's more design-conscious acquaintances were aghast at this. Other restaurateurs spend fortunes trying to open walls up to the street—and in a listed SoHo building, you can't just punch a hole in the wall when and where you feel like it. But what McNally cares passionately about is not views of the street, but the shape, feel, and above all the coziness of the Great Indoors. "I find restaurants with 'views' quite ridiculous to begin with," says McNally flatly. "It's the food and the people I'm with that matters. And if I'm going to be looking anywhere else, it's probably at others across the room who might seem to be having a better time than myself."

McNally first discovered the space, at 80 Spring Street, in the fall of 1995. "It was a dilapidated and cobwebbed leather wholesale store. The interior was an impossible warren of small rooms, each stuffed to the rafters with more scraps of leather than the last, and run by some ancient orthodox Jew and his family. The basement was a separate entity: a sweatshop full of foreign-speaking seamstresses, each paid about twenty cents a day."

Riad Nasr vividly remembers the first time he saw the space. McNally, whom he didn't know, rang out of the blue and said that he was thinking of starting a new restaurant; would he come and have a look at the place? Nasr and Lee Hanson, having forged a strong friendship in the kitchens of Daniel Boulud, had been thinking of striking out on their own.

But capital was short, and work with McNally, whose entrepreneurial spirit had already been shown with the success of other restaurants, seemed a possible intermediary step. So the two met at the space, but there was practically nothing there. "Then Keith pulled a photo out of his pocket. It was dog-eared and wrinkled, and what you saw was this anonymous brasserie bar somewhere in France. That's all it was. Just a bar with a wall behind it, but Keith was in raptures. In fact I think it was the last time I saw him smile. But I did at least think that this is a man who really cares about detail. And, for better or worse, I jumped on board."

McNally doesn't work with professional designers or interior decorators ("You must be joking!"), but in putting Balthazar together (he hates the word "design") he worked in unison with friend, designer, and contractor Ian McPheely. "I come up with an idea, then Ian comes up with a better one and puts it immediately into practice. Apart from being modest and talented, he's also able to make something out of the one object I always begin a project with. The look of each restaurant is triggered by me becoming totally fixated on one item that I think will make or break the place. I then research this thing more or less to death. At Pravda it was a 1920s metal street lamp I'd seen in Poland. At Pastis, a turn-of-the-century institutional wall tile. And at Balthazar, a faded photo of an old bar from somewhere in France." The bar was flanked by a pair of zaftig female caryatids, which McNally obsessed about. Where could such creatures be found? It would be impossible, of course, to discover the originals, lost with the original brasserie. Unable to find anything like them in the flea markets he haunted in Paris, he eventually got a sculptor from Brooklyn, Brandt Junceau, to copy them from the photo. For models, Junceau used two handsome-breasted waitresses from Pravda. Now they reign over the bar like Belle Epoque goddesses, their plaster skin yellowed and looking more than a century old, as though they really had been made when Picasso was an infant.

The doors of Balthazar open at 7:30 and the first clients of the day, most of them somewhat bleary-eyed and unwilling to be disturbed by waiter or God, arrive for their coffee, newspapers, and boiled, poached, or scrambled eggs. The favorite standard is eggs Benedict, whose elements get prepared well in advance: dozens of soft-poached eggs kept by the side of the stove in a basin of hot water, so that they stay warm but don't cook any further; a container of hollandaise sauce. It takes only a New York minute to slide a couple of these onto the halves of a lightly toasted English muffin and slather them with hollandaise, so the cook can serve out an eggs Benedict faster than he can fry an egg. It is not, despite what some clients think, a time-consuming dish, so long as its elements are prepped in advance—one of the fundamental characteristics of brasserie cooking. But first thing in the morning, other than croissants and brioches (produced in Balthazar's own bakery), eggs and endless cups of coffee are the main order of the day.

The morning wears away and breakfast becomes lunch: the second wave of the day, when the pressure of the kitchen, its staff, and the floor workers starts to become intense. Though one cannot be too precise about it, it starts around noon, when the full lunch menu —say ten hors d'oeuvres, four or five salads for the light eaters, a half-dozen sandwiches, and ten main courses—has to be ready to roll out.

It's now that the pecking order of the restaurant, its structure of authority, starts to be fully apparent—though not to the customers in the dining room, who are happily ignorant of it. Everyone backstage is fully engaged, from the dishwashers who are feeding the enormous machines to the assistant patissier who is busy burning the crusts of sugar on the crèmes brûlées—a task that used to be done by sliding a whole rack of them under a top-mounted grill or salamander, but at Balthazar is done more prosaically and accurately with a little hissing propane torch of the kind used by plumbers. Restaurants, as anyone knows who has worked in one, are not democracies. They are pure hierarchy, top to bottom. They are unfair by nature. In McNally's words: there is always extreme friction between the kitchen and the floor. "The kitchen is one of the few workplaces left in the world where political correctness doesn't have a prayer: it's unquestionably a masculine place." And yet solidarity and loyalty between the chef and his cooks is incomparable, and it isn't a matter of formal unionism. "During a mad moment, Riad might yell his lungs out at a cook, but if someone from outside the kitchen even remotely criticizes that cook, he'll be out on his ear, instantly."

The pressure climbs toward lunchtime, levels off around three, and then with early evening goes up again, reaching a climax of intensity at about nine o'clock. But the place is still serving at two A.M., and sometimes at three. This follows an instinctive preference of McNally's: a brasserie has to close, but for as short a time as reasonably possible. It has to be a sort of home away from home. In practice, of course, this isn't possible. But it is comforting to know that you can get really good steak frites at two in the morning. And where else can you do it in downtown New York?

And so it goes at the brasserie. A brasserie is not a bistro. Bistros are small, which is part of their charm. Brasseries can be big: witness the famous La Coupole at 102 Boulevard du Montparnasse, the famed and demotic eating house to which Parisians and tourists have flocked for decades, with its frescoes by the long-departed Fauvist Othon Friesz. La Coupole is probably larger, consistent with decent food, than any restaurant in the world. One often hears Balthazar spoken of as New York's equivalent to La Coupole, but the comparison is very inexact, as between the *Mauretania* and a fair-sized yacht. Beside La Coupole, Balthazar is a quite modest operation: La Coupole has 500 seats and can serve several thousand "covers"—complete meals—a day, while Balthazar can seat 180. This is large but not vast. "On a busy Saturday or Sunday," McNally says "we'll seat about 800 people for brunch, 500 for dinner, and with the addition of breakfast and supper, the total will come to about 1,500 covers."

What Balthazar and La Coupole do have in common, however, is that they are not elaborate restaurants, but brasseries—businesses that sell classically simple food, reliable standards that everyone (or almost everyone) likes to eat. Brasserie cooking is straightforward and conservative, and McNally is totally devoted to it. It is his idea of heaven, and it suggests (to him) implications of social utopia that are altogether lacking (for him) in the more elaborate and formal rituals of eating. It is not a field of experiment, at least not in

France, however unfamiliar it may have seemed when it first came to America. It does not depend on elaborate sauces or numerous stages of preparation.

Generally, the food is straight down the middle of the road, and all the more liked for it. In the same way, the restaurant's wine list is straightforward, tending to shun the precious and overpriced top end and going for more affordable growths and vintages. It concentrates mainly on medium-ticket French wines, of which they sell about a thousand bottles weekly. The cellar is in one of the subterranean rooms, where the old ladies chatting in Yiddish used to toil, stacked to the ceiling no longer with leather off-cuts but with wine crates. Most of the wines are priced at $30 to $50, with carafes at less than $20. There are more expensive Bordeaux, some even as high as $600 to $800, but McNally is less than comfortable with these. "It's necessary to have a range of wines. But the very expensive ones terrify me. Besides, my palate dulls at anything over $50."

Balthazar tries to keep its prices at a level that, if not rock bottom, are at least realistic for most diners: at lunch, a *frisée aux lardons* for $10; an unctuously creamy *brandade de morue* (purée of salt cod and potatoes, crusted under the salamander) for $7.50. The most expensive main course is often a *plat du jour*, such as Sunday's cassoulet or Saturday's short ribs, topping out at $25. We are a long way from the $35 and even $60 entrées offered by the chefs of more luxurious establishments, like Daniel Boulud or, at a much further extreme, the Parisian chef-entrepreneur Alain Ducasse, whose restaurant opened in New York in 2000 to less than ecstatic reviews from critics who, understandably, could not comprehend his prices.

The most expensive dish on Balthazar's menu is its eponymous seafood platter, Le Balthazar, at $99. But this is not a one-person dish. It's enormous, not a platter but a three-story marine tower of Babel, like something from the easel of a seventeenth-century Dutch still-life artist, its metal supporting frame fairly creaking under the weight of ice, clams, razor clams, mussels, cockles, winkles, small whole crabs, stone-crab claws, and half a smallish lobster. Less a dish than a mise-en-scène, it is one of the few dishes I have ever seen in a New York restaurant that conveys some impression, however slight, of the way that at least some of the ancestors of the present clientele might have eaten back in the days of Tammany Hall, those lost times when Canal Street really was a saltwater canal, and oysters—reputedly, if scarcely credibly, the size of dessert plates—were raked from its silt, and American gargantuans like Diamond Jim Brady, with their gold watch chains resembling the anchor chains of coastal freighters, would engulf six dozen or more of them before settling down to the serious business of lobster, sturgeon, and beefsteak. Such men would scarcely have regarded the three tiers of Le Balthazar as more than a speck on the road to satiation.

Some people may find my loyalty to Balthazar almost unnatural. But in 1970, when I moved to the tract of downtown Manhattan that in a few years' time would be christened SoHo, there was practically nowhere in the vicinity to eat. Thirty years later, the idea seems barely credible. But back then SoHo was a whole neighborhood with no name, no development, and no restaurant that was halfway decent. It was possible to eat, in a minimal sort of way. You could get chili at the bar of Fanelli's on the corner of Prince and

Mercer—you still can, and commendable it is. You could get pasta and *sott'aceti* at another Italian joint on Prince.

Then, through the seventies, a variety of small restaurants with aspirations to somewhat higher cuisine appeared in the cavernous ground-floor spaces of the loft buildings. All, for one reason or another, folded.

What SoHo needed, but did not have, was something like La Coupole in Paris: a place where its burgeoning population of artists, dancers, journalists, and tourists could go to feed; somewhere large and comfortable, with good food, to catch the runoff from the culture industry that was growing between Houston and Canal Streets. A place that would help give the idea of a *style du quartier* some kind of concrete expression, and do it on a fairly large scale. And on a large scale it did: the 12,000 working square feet of Balthazar's restaurant and bakery opened in April 1997. In its first year it served more than a quarter of a million meals, a number that has increased with each passing year.

Whether it will continue, I have no idea. I hope it will stay open forever. But then, that's what New Yorkers said and thought about the Stork Club, Toots Shor's, El Morocco, and any number of watering- and eating-holes that were once considered part of the essence of New York and are now only a memory, indistinctly preserved in old press photos and black-and-white movies. Some day, unlikely as this may seem, even the Four Seasons will serve its last $35 hamburger (which will probably cost $60 and still, allowing for inflation, be worth it to at least some people). In the meantime, Balthazar remains essential for those of us who live wedded to downtown, and for quite a few who do not. It has deeply affected the rituals and habits of eating in the neighborhood. At the same time, it is not merely a "neighborhood" restaurant. It's not that you can't imagine SoHo without it. Things have moved on from there: You can't imagine New York without it.

Like so many things in Manhattan, Balthazar was invented, and continues to be sustained, by an Englishman. Perhaps this had to be so: perhaps only an Englishman—and a working-class Englishman at that—could have short-circuited the peculiar and irritating form of the restaurant snobbery that tended to deface the experience of eating out in New York.

Born under the sign of Leo on July 30, 1951, in the working-class London suburb of Bethnal Green, Keith McNally was the third son of a stevedore and a charlady. For most of his life, McNally's father worked on the London docks, loading and unloading cargo. He was "wildly inarticulate and interested in few things outside of soccer, but decent beyond." McNally *père*, now eighty-two, lives contentedly with his son and daughter-in-law on Eleventh Street in Greenwich Village, keeping busy four days a week by folding napkins at Balthazar —"A job," says Keith with his usual slightly morose twinkle, "that requires thirty-five years on the London docks to do properly."

Keith's mother was more interested—much more—in the life of the mind, and it was from her that McNally's interest in books and theater came. As working-class as her husband, she read avidly; at the age of forty, she taught herself to speak and read Spanish, of which he, by contrast, understood not a syllable. She began as an office cleaner and ended up with "a clerical position of minor distinction" at London's General Post Office. "They weren't the happiest of couples," McNally recalls. "In fact I never once saw them touch each other, but as they produced four children I have to assume they did. What I did witness, however, and without letup, was the two of them arguing. It seemed to happen every day of the week, with Christmas and weddings being their forte. With this in mind, it's quite peculiar that I'm in the hospitality business, for anything less hospitable than the home I grew up in would be hard to imagine. However, my parents were subjected far more than I ever was to the awful class system in England, and knowing this, it's a miracle how adequately they provided for us."

Neither parent had any connection with food, beyond making and eating it at home, and eating out at a restaurant was just something the family never did. But McNally vividly remembers the first time he did, and it wasn't with his parents. The year was 1968 (year of revolution! year of upheaval!) and he was seventeen, on the cusp between being a young actor and a real one, working in a play by Alan Bennett, called *Forty Years On*, in a West End theater. Some of the cast went round the corner to have dinner after the night's performance, to a reliable Italian restaurant named Bianchi's, in Soho. There McNally ordered melon (or it was ordered for him). "It was the first time I'd ever eaten—or seen—a melon. The problem was I didn't know where to stop eating it, and ended up going through the skin and onto the plate."

The acting was important. McNally did not go to university. He passed a tough test called the Eleven Plus and was streamed into a good-quality and rigorous grammar school that, he claims, "did a monumental job at teaching me how to avoid homework, schoolwork, and just about any kind of work." At fifteen he wrote an essay that "somehow got squeezed into a pool of essays by other London teenagers," and he was asked to both read and talk about it on BBC Radio. Instead of being paralyzed with terror, he relished the experience. This led to a brief life in the theater, until at nineteen he began an extended *Wanderjahr*, walking off, hitchhiking and traveling as far from England as possible. For a time, in 1971, he worked on a kibbutz in Israel. He then went by thumb, trains, and local trucks through Turkey, Iran, and Afghanistan, spending the best part of a year in Kathmandu and India. This was a time before war and the terrors of religious bigotry closed down the frontiers of the Middle East. And this was the kind of education by travel that would hardly be possible for a Westerner in today's nightmarish political world.

Keith McNally would never be an English provincial again. In 1975 he left London, without green card or papers, for New York, and there found himself a job as a busboy in a curious hybrid of teashop and boutique named Serendipity on Sixtieth Street in Manhattan. From there he moved on, but as a waiter, to the now defunct Maxwell's Plum, an extravagantly decorated Belle Epoque restaurant owned by Warner LeRoy, a rotund, cackling, hail-fellow-well-met host with strong Hollywood and other showbiz connections and an insatiable taste for Tiffanoid décor. As a waiter McNally did not exactly thrive. "I was terrible because I could never remember orders. I would listen to a customer ask for something, but by the time I got back to the kitchen I'd forgotten what it was. Then in bed at three in the morning, I'd suddenly wake up remembering it. Luckily I left before I was fired." Then he began work at One Fifth, a new restaurant that had just opened downtown at Eighth Street and Fifth Avenue. It was relatively small, not a mass affair like Maxwell's Plum, more on the scale of a bistro than a brasserie, "but in its own way quite beautiful," with its frosted glass and Art Deco light fixtures. "It had the kind of style a lot of people—myself included—had never seen before. The food was nothing to write home, or anywhere else, about. But the look and atmosphere somehow transported you. It was a very thrilling place to work." Which McNally did for four years, starting out as an oyster shucker and then working his way up to general manager.

In 1980, with his then-girlfriend, Lynn Wagenknecht, and brother Brian, he put together his first restaurant, the Odeon. It had originally been built as a cafeteria in the late 1930s, and it had a distinct architectural style—working-class Deco, as it were—that McNally thought (correctly) would have been madness to change. At that time such places were common below Canal Street; today they are unfindable. With its huge, red neon CAFETERIA sign outside, the Odeon opened in what was to many the most desolate spot in the city, TriBeCa. But within two or three days, people were finding their way there. "It brought a lot of people downtown, including quite a few local artists." This is an understatement from McNally. Once in a blue moon a restaurant will appear that creates a grateful clientele almost overnight. So it was with the Odeon—it really had no competition. All of a sudden, TriBeCa had its bonsai Coupole, presided over by a rotund but temperamental genius, an African-American cook named Patrick Clark. Clark did not believe that a restaurant in Odeon's then-unpromising territory could truly succeed, but after the third night the place was packed to the rafters and has remained so ever since. What hasn't is McNally's ownership of the place. Like his second venture, Café Luxembourg, and his third, Nell's, Odeon is now owned by ex-wife Lynn. "I don't own it but I still very much enjoy going there. The problem is I now get a check."

It is late Thursday afternoon, the last lunchers have gone, and McNally and his staff are having their weekly bull session, going over the running of the restaurant. This usually includes The Sermon: McNally on what may, for want of a better term, be called the ideals of Balthazar.

"The restaurant's success hinges on customers leaving happier than when they arrived. It's that simple. And our job begins the second that customer comes in the door. No, the maître d' can't be on the phone, with his back to the door, or talking to the attractive hostess. He's got to instantly acknowledge the guest the moment that person enters the restaurant. Remember, it's intimidating walking into a busy place like this. *You* might be comfortable here, but the customer coming in for the first time is decidedly *not.* Whatever your position in the restaurant, always put yourself in the customer's shoes, that's all I'm asking."

The man in charge of the front of the house is Michael LaHara, the general manager, a taciturn but all-noticing Italian-American in his late forties. He doesn't take care of the intake of raw materials, but everything that goes wrong (or right) between Balthazar and its clients falls under his purview. "Reservations, cancellations, holidays, planning ahead, reviewing the menus." If a client starts getting obstreperous, the task of dealing with him falls to LaHara—not that LaHara is any sort of bouncer. But sometimes they do act up: pretending to have reservations they never made, jabbing their fingers in the faces of the reservation-takers and the maître d'. It's at that point that the normally invisible, or at least unnoticed, LaHara makes himself felt, though in practice it's almost never necessary to bodily eject an angry customer. Generally the worst that comes along—and that, not so often—is a bum who stakes out his territory on one of the benches in front of the brasserie, or who starts accosting and panhandling clients on the way in or out. LaHara deals with this by calling the cops, who come fast, though usually it's enough just to let the panhandler know they're on the way.

At the other end of the scale of welcome, LaHara emphatically denies that Balthazar keeps a favorites list. "What Keith says is quite true: if he favors anyone, it's the couple at the back of the queue who seem a bit uncertain, who don't look confident of being seated. But of course there are regulars, and are you supposed to ignore a regular, or treat him like a stranger? I don't think so."

LaHara consults on food with Keith and the chefs, Riad and Lee. "We're always having to deal with what I'd call love-hate items. Mussels, for instance. Some people can't stand them. And yet they're classic brasserie food, and more people than you think want to see them on the menu. The same with, let's say, tripe." But LaHara's view of the restaurant, so to speak, is global. "It starts when I come in, about 7:30 in the morning. A lot of people have already been on the job for hours, and I start visually checking it all. Uniforms: dirty, clean, sloppy, crisp? Debris still on the floor from the night before? Lighting? Even simple chores like acknowledging every one of the staff, which helps individuals feel like part of a team. You can't leave any of the day-to-day stuff out, because that has an effect on morale and it puts you out of touch. And being in touch is exactly what Keith pays me for."

Typically, the New York restaurant at a certain level of effort and expense tends, no matter how much denial it injects into it, to be an exercise in status-snobbery. And some New Yorkers will put up with any discomfort—from mere drafts to ritual humiliation—in order to be seen doing the right thing at the right place. In the eighties it didn't matter how powerful they might be in their own fields of influence. They might direct the destinies of handbags or of real estate. No matter. Their fate was in the hands of the doorman or reservations clerk, who could permit or deny access in the most arbitrary way. And as often as not, they went because the purpose of going was to prove they could get in. The fashionable disco or restaurant of the 1980s, buoyed up by breathless articles in *New York* magazine and elsewhere, became a tool for forcing the nouveaus to whom time was money to squander time itself. Hence the long, irksome, and humiliating waits at the bar, to be seated at ten for a nine reservation; hence the flat refusal, by some restaurants, to let the client sit down at the reserved and visibly empty table before the "whole party" had arrived. The passive willingness to comply with these tyrannies-from-below has long been thought an index of a restaurant's success. It hasn't anything to do with the quality of the food, although the New York clientele is much more discerning about what it eats than it was a quarter-century ago.

And because so many New Yorkers are fixated celebrity-hounds, they will tend to cluster in places whose clientele they have read about and hope to glimpse across the room.

Now, there's no denying that Balthazar is a fashionable restaurant. But it doesn't behave like one. It doesn't exploit masochism. Despite the flood of publicity in the months that followed its opening in April of 1997, despite the odd rumors that pumped its reputation for exclusivity, such as the stories of secret reservation phone numbers and even numbers-within-numbers, it is not, in fact, unusually difficult to get a table there, except at the last moment on Friday or Saturday night, which is only to be expected. And no table seems to have more cachet than any other, except for the booths along the east wall. Certainly there are no tables that brand their occupants as inferior beings lacking in clout and unknown to the management. This lack of a Siberia is one of the nicest things about Balthazar, and it is connected to the deepest nature and social belief of its owner. Balthazar reflects, as all restaurants (good, bad, or in between) inevitably do, the character of its owner-manager and cooks: in this case, Keith McNally, Lee Hanson, and Riad Nasr. McNally is not a snob. He is a genuine and instinctive democrat, and that is where the popularity of his restaurant starts: in its straightforwardness. This quality used to be quite rare amongst American and particularly New York restaurateurs, who were apt to regard themselves (if they could get away with it) as social as well as gastronomic mentors. It remains common even today. The snotty headwaiter peering disdainfully down his nose at the unknown client is by no means a creature of the past.

McNally has never allowed a restaurant he owns to be run this way. There are several reasons for this. The compelling one is that he hates snobbery—and would not let his staff put on the dog. "I think," he reflects, "that coming from a poor family in an acutely class-ridden society leaves its mark. Snobbery, of any kind, repulses me. If the restaurant works, it's because it appeals to different kinds of people from truly diverse backgrounds. Arrogance and pretension are the last things a customer wants to put up with when entering a restaurant. Apart from the technical skills, the only things I ask of my staff are to be decent and normal, that's all."

It is an oldish question, but not perhaps a very interesting one, whether cooking is an art or not. It used not to be. There is little creative about tossing a snake or a deer's haunch on the embers of a fire. Certainly, in the order of creativity, it ranks a good deal lower than drawing a bison on a rock. But then cooking got more complex in its materials, methods, ingredients, and presentation. It developed not just a present, but a history, or rather innumerable histories. As these histories grew and interwove, they took on a creative character and produced things that weren't there before. These "things" made form from chaos, by appealing to the senses.

It is pretentious to talk about cuisine having an intellectual dimension, the way writing or painting necessarily have. But it exists under the auspices of its own history, a trait that it has in common with other activities called art. No tradition, no comparison; no comparison, no art. All cooking is extremely tradition-conscious, and there are only a limited number of things you can do with any ingredient: bake it, boil it, simmer it, fry it, serve it raw, and so on. Perhaps the taste buds are not as receptive to infinite nuances and degrees of stimulus as our eye-brain linkages. In any case, it is no longer much of a compliment to call an activity "art," given some of the garbage that gets exhibited in galleries and museums in the early twenty-first century. An art like what exactly?

Not every cook deserves to be called a chef—a term that in any case boils down to very little. No wonder that both Lee Hanson and Riad Nasr, talking about their work at Balthazar, emphasize, "We don't ever have an elevated view of our job. Certainly we never think of it as something approaching art." Craft, it is. Skill too. They see themselves as highly skilled craftsmen to whom the idea of "invention" is the merest red herring. Besides, as Nasr points out, the range of sensation, feeling, and—if you want to use the word—*meaning* presented by food is much narrower than that of the high arts. Food is about pleasure and nothing but pleasure. Nobody wants food (if you can imagine such food) that makes you feel miserable. Cooking has no tragic dimension; it cannot—to invoke the classical Greek definition of tragedy—purge the soul through pity and terror. At least, one hopes not. But cooking is also too important a business to have the presently debased word "art" attached to it. There is no Kandinsky of cuisine, nor should there be.

At heart, McNally is absolutely a Francophile. He loves French food, and French ambience no less. The very idea of sitting in an ordinary French restaurant sends him into ecstasies of recollection. "I like French restaurants certainly, but what gravitates me toward France are the cafés. Sitting, reading a newspaper for hours on end with a constant refill of dark rich coffee—the sheer, unadulterated laziness of it. And it was this memory of café laziness that I had very much in mind when building Balthazar. I just feel lucky that the culinary side is in the hands of Riad and Lee. Besides possessing an inordinate amount of skill, they understand the philosophy of the place, and that's crucial if it's going to work. I think our dedication to the job is pretty similar, as is our suspicion of anyone with a trace of self-importance. Riad and Lee are as unpretentious as they are hardworking, and that's probably why we get along so well." Lee Hanson agrees: "No one here talks about the restaurant or the food in terms of design or concept. We try to be as straightforward as we can. And though we're passionate about cooking the food, no one in the kitchen believes we're creating the Sistine Chapel, and nor would I want them to."

Every time McNally opens a restaurant there is always a flurry in the press about how it's the hottest new ticket, the most difficult thing to get into. How does he square this with what he is saying? He reacts with something close to defensive weariness. "I don't have a PR person, I don't court the press, and I'm not in the dining room shaking hands with the customers. Most of my time is spent with the chefs, the general manager, and meetings with the staff. I don't own restaurants to advance socially, and I shun most of the few social events I'm invited to. I'm not saying I'm a Trappist monk, it's just that I don't turn cartwheels at the idea of meeting new people. I respect those who come to the restaurant and in fact feel fortunate that as many come as often as they do. I'm also conscious of the kind of fashionable New Yorker who goes only to new restaurants, and those customers are the ones I see the second I open a new place and then never again three months afterward. But that's okay, everything has its place. I just no longer get bowled over if the restaurant is full on day one with somewhat glamorous people. It's a cliché, but it's five or so years down the line that matters, when those people are long past making the headlines and even longer past coming in through the doors of my restaurant. But of course if the staff isn't doing their job, these customers would never come in the first place. That's why the majority of my time is spent reiterating the same points to every member of my staff. In particular I can't tolerate waiters who are either rude or pretentious or who self-importantly recite the day's specials in the first-person singular ("Today I have…').

"I may be critical of my staff, but ultimately I'm much closer to them than the customers. In fact so many of them do jobs that I patently couldn't do, I'm almost in awe of them. Particularly those in the kitchen. I see what pressure they're under and how hard they work, and immediately I'm reminded of how little I contribute to the restaurant's success. I feel particularly distant from its workings when I enter the restaurant after a few days' absence. It's then that I see it as I imagine a customer sees it: huge platters of shellfish shuttled through a bustling dining room. Bartenders mixing vodka martinis. Captains, waiters, and busboys crisscrossing a crowded, animated room. All that's alive and vital about New York, and the reason why I came here in the first place."

Watching the human machinery going on a good day, the choreography of a very crowded room, one is put in mind of what was once said about Charles Dickens: that his novels sold so well not because he *knew* what his public wanted, but because he *wanted* what his public wanted. There was no angle between the desires of the maker and those of the reader—or, in this case, the eater. This is not something that can be feigned. And it seems to be true of McNally and his staff today. He would never upgrade a brasserie, in the sense of making it more luxurious, more ostentatious or expensive, more difficult of access. He has the clientele he wants, in the kind of brasserie he likes best to eat in. Balthazar is an end in itself, not a step toward something else. And this is why it has brilliantly and durably succeeded where so many others have failed.

Given its large size and continuous, booming business, you would think running Balthazar was enough for one man. But McNally has others: Pravda a few blocks away on Lafayette, Pastis over in the downtown meatpacking district, Lucky Strike on Grand Street in SoHo. He is also planning another downtown restaurant. But at present, Balthazar is the flagship.

Restaurants rise and sink. They start out promising or grandly, sometimes surrounded by great pink clouds of fluffy hype, sometimes creeping almost unnoticed at first onto the horizon. But they rarely last long unless they manage to root themselves in some deep culinary need, something that their city lacked, sometimes almost without knowing it. Some are grand and ambitious and, what is more, actually deliver on what look like suicidal pretensions. At the other end of the scale, others are merely idiotic, geared to fleeting notions of celebrity but having nothing to do with food. Among New York restaurants, there is a huge and variegated menu of failure.

Balthazar did not fail, and in the course of its survival became a fixture in many lives, including my own. Almost from the day it opened, it became the best brasserie in New York City or, for that matter, in America. It is, in a real sense, a restaurateur's restaurant: asked where he normally eats (other than his own place, Daniel, which is one of the most esteemed high-end restaurants in New York), Daniel Boulud, for whom both Riad Nasr and Lee Hanson used to work, unhesitatingly invokes the name *Balthazar*.

SoHo, New York
2003

THE

BALTHAZAR
COOKBOOK

THE

BALTHAZAR
COOKBOOK

by

KEITH McNALLY,
RIAD NASR & LEE HANSON

with KATHRYN KELLINGER

Foreword .... **Robert Hughes**

Photographs by ...... **Christopher Hirsheimer** & **Ron Haviv**

Clarkson Potter/Publishers

— NEW YORK —

PUBLISHED BY

Clarkson Potter/Publishers
— NEW YORK, NEW YORK —

Member of the Crown Publishing Group, a division of Random House, Inc.
www.randomhouse.com
Clarkson N. Potter is a trademark and POTTER and colophon
are registered trademarks of Random House, Inc.

DESIGN BY MATTEO BOLOGNA AND VICTOR MINGOVITS
for MUCCA DESIGN

Printed in Hong Kong

Library of Congress Cataloging-in-Publication Data
McNally, Keith.
The Balthazar cookbook / Keith McNally, Riad Nasr, and Lee Hanson;
foreword by Robert Hughes; photographs by Christopher Hirsheimer.
1. Cookery, French.   I. Nasr, Riad.   II. Hanson, Lee.   III. Title.
TX719 .M397   2003
641.5944—dc21   2002154175

ISBN 1-4000-4635-1

10   9

FIRST EDITION

— CONTENTS —

$$\frac{}{}$$

— INTRODUCTION —

In describing how Balthazar came about, I'd like to recall an early family holiday in the south of France where I experienced my first taste of foie gras. I'd like to, but it'd be a complete lie. My childhood was spent in a drab working-class section of London in the 1950s; France, known then as the Continent, was about as distant as the Pyramids. Equally distant was the prospect of eating in a restaurant. It was something my family just didn't do. Partly from cost, but also from the somewhat inhibiting effects of the English class system. My parents were from a generation who "knew their place," and a restaurant, particularly a French one, was clearly *not* their place. But even if they had summoned the courage to enter a restaurant, the process of public dining—seating, ordering, even eating—would have terrorized them. It would have seemed like a ritual understood by everyone in the dining room except themselves. And for the rest of the family—my sister, two brothers, and myself—it would have been an embarrassment bordering on humiliation.

This meant that for my first sixteen years I ate either at school or at home. At school, food was about as pleasurable as calculus. At home, my mother cooked, determinedly and without argument, only one of two ways: Boiled or Baked. So when at sixteen I traveled to Paris for the weekend, food was the last thing on my mind. The first and only thing was a horse race. I'd gone there to put a year's worth of savings on a horse in what was then the richest race in the world, the Prix de l'Arc de Triomphe. Of course, my horse lost, and with it went my spirits, my savings, and an opportunity to eat my first meal in a French restaurant. Broke and at a low ebb, I loathed France, its people, and its annoyingly fast racehorses. I trudged back to my pensione and vowed never to have anything to do with the place again.

A year after leaving school I drifted into the English theater. The one play I passed an audition for was in the West End, so I found myself working in an area bursting with the kinds of restaurants from which I'd always felt excluded. And though being an actor now gave me the confidence to enter these places, that confidence vanished the second I was presented a menu—in English of course, but I could barely understand a word of it: artichokes, avocados, leeks, endives, squash—even the simplest ingredients were lost on me. I'd grown up in a post-war working-class environment where stomachs, not palettes, mattered. And by seventeen the only vegetables I'd ever eaten were peas, spinach, and Brussels sprouts. This often meant that as I peered at a menu my eyes would take on the glazed look of someone staring at a very complex exam paper for which he hadn't prepared. The food's arrival was no less taxing. I remember being served an artichoke and not having a clue in the world as to how to eat it. And then came the silverware. Having to choose only one utensil from what seemed like a battalion was just mortifying. All I could ever do was guess. But that guess was based not on trying to choose the right utensil, but rather the one that would prove least embarrassing if wrong. It's how most of my decisions are still made, I'm afraid, for embarrassment terrifies me. If this weren't so, I could perhaps have enjoyed those first few visits to French restaurants. Instead, I spent every second covering up my ignorance. And worse, at the end of it I still had to pay the check.

After my year-long stint in the theater I left England to hitchhike around Europe, Afghanistan, and India. I'd like to say I dropped acid and discovered enlightenment, but I did neither. I washed dishes, picked oranges, and traveled to Kathmandu and back with the rare achievement of not experiencing one memorable incident. This was more than made up for when I returned to England and managed a women's strip club in Wardour Street, Soho. Working night after night with beautiful naked women, one becomes totally immune to their bodies. One does, but I didn't. Far from it. This was the best job I'd had in my life, and I was going to hold on to it for as long as possible. Unfortunately that wasn't long at all, as I soon got fired. It was then that I decided to pack my one bag and head off for New York.

I arrived in Manhattan in 1975 with the lofty intention of writing and directing films. A week later I was clearing plates and setting tables as an illegally hired busboy. Drudgery for others, perhaps, but exhilarating for me. Not only was I finally comfortable in a restaurant, but I was working smack in the center of New York City. Intoxicated, I immediately gave up on the film idea. It was the fast lane of bussing tables or nothing. A succession of restaurant jobs led to my sole kitchen experience as a clam and oyster opener at a restaurant in Greenwich Village called One Fifth. Its Art Deco interior was rescued from an ocean liner, and its opening in January 1976 caused quite a stir. It was stylish and hip and had reasonable food, but crucial to its success was its association with downtown. Crucial to *my* success was the fact that it was so chronically mismanaged that after a series of firings, walkouts, and more firings, I was the only one standing who could be called upon to run the place. This I did, with mixed results, for four years.

It was during this time that I met Lynn Wagenknecht (later to be my wife, then my ex-wife), and together we often traveled to Paris. On one of these trips, the two of us decided to try to build a restaurant of our own. Along with my brother, we took over an old cafeteria in TriBeCa, and after six months of renovations opened the Odeon; this was in the fall of 1980. It was promptly followed by marriage and three other restaurants. Then in 1989 I took time off to write and direct an independent feature film, *End of the Night*. Though selected for the Cannes Film Festival and distributed in a number of countries, it was not exactly a megahit. Nor even a minor one. However, decent reviews in Europe prompted various producers to commission another script. To write and direct it, I moved with my wife and three children to Paris for two years.

These were the worst two years of my life. The film was a disaster, my marriage collapsed, and I fell apart at the seams and everywhere else. On poor advice I then went and sold my half of the Odeon to my wife, plus two of the three remaining restaurants. In the space of a couple of months I seemed to have lost everything. But I did at least eat well. Not at Michelin-blessed restaurants where ingredients came artfully arranged on oversized plates, but at cheap and overcrowded bistros where food was served without ceremony and yet tasted as delicious as anything in the city: cassoulet, coquilles St.-Jacques, sole meunière, blanquette de veau, brandade, escargot, hanger steak with french fries, and Brittany oysters by the bucketful. Separated and depressed, I ate everything the city's bistros had to offer, and I discovered that in the process of losing one attachment, I had involuntarily gained another. With divorce and bistro food on my mind, I returned to New York to start over again. I suppose this is where Balthazar began.

Although I was initially unsure of its look, the underlying idea behind Balthazar was always clear. It was to be a large, graciously bustling restaurant that reflected downtown Manhattan as well as the more obliging aspects of French brasseries. These included late hours, modest prices, and an unprejudiced sense of accommodation. I had in mind a place where one could be transported without being intimidated. Where the service was unconditionally free of snobbery and that hideous restaurant practice of describing the day's specials without offering a price. Most of all I wanted to serve the kind of unfussy bistro food I'd devoured day after day in Paris. But before any of this could be done, I had to first find a location and start building.

Eighty Spring Street was formerly a leather wholesaler's—an unfathomable maze of airless rooms stacked floor to ceiling with scraps of leather. Only after emptying out its contents and knocking down the walls did I know exactly what I'd rented. If only I'd also known what I'd *wanted* I could have saved hundreds of thousands of dollars. But I didn't. I don't work that way. Unfortunately for the schedule and budget, I never begin a restaurant with a blueprint of the finished product. Partly because I rarely know what I want the finished product to be, and partly because I'm unsure that it'd be good for the restaurant if I did. Instead I grab on to some peculiar detail that I'm convinced is crucial to getting the whole thing airborne. With Balthazar it was a black-and-white photograph of an old, anonymous Parisian bar. I didn't have a clue how to build the restaurant's interior: its kitchen, oyster bar, booths, banquettes, bathrooms, entranceway, wine room, and so on. But I felt that if I could build a bar with the look or spirit of the one in the photograph, then somehow everything else would fall into place.

I couldn't have been more wrong. The bar *did* begin to be built, but little fell into place, and what did put me way over budget. Six months into the project, I was a million dollars over budget and four months behind schedule. But I had only myself to blame. My obsession with details meant that we were progressing at a snail's pace. The problem was that even though my ideas were only half formed, they were still head and shoulders above my abilities. And were it not for the more able hands of co-designer (and contractor) Ian McPheely, I'd still be in the same confusion I was then. But I was at least accumulating furniture: from Philadelphia, old mahogany paneling and vast sheets of distressed mirror; from French flea markets, tables, chairs, shelving, coat hooks, and light fixtures. I also found a factory near Paris willing to cast a thirty-five-foot pewter bar.

Although the look of Balthazar was taking its cue from the turn-of-the-century photograph, I would constantly bristle at the suggestion I was building a "period" restaurant. I'm anti-"period" most things, including restaurants, but this doesn't prevent me from gravitating toward the kinds of materials and regard for detail that I find more prevalent in restaurant interiors built before World War II. Particularly European ones. But simply reproducing the interior of another period is anathema to me, as it usually results in nothing more than an artificial stage set. With its strong attachment to downtown Manhattan, I think and hope Balthazar is more than this; but being its owner, I suppose I'm not altogether in a position to judge. Besides, it wasn't brasseries I was imagining while building the place, but cafés. Parisian cafés where I'd wasted entire afternoons lingering over coffee and newspapers. It was the atmosphere of such places, not the precise look of them, that I was most interested in.

But appearances would mean little if I didn't have a chef, and six months into the project I still hadn't found one. Through ads and other restaurateurs, I met various potential chefs. Whenever an interview went well, I'd take matters a step further by asking for a private tasting. Being cooked exclusively for in this way was quite a treat, but the process was too much like an uncomfortable date to really enjoy. Then a friend mentioned a brilliant but taciturn young cook, Riad Nasr, who was Daniel Boulud's sous-chef. A day or so later I agreed to meet him. In walked this unsmiling samurai warrior figure who said so little, and understated his skills to such a degree, that by comparison I felt oddly inadequate. That's probably why I wanted to hire him. But first I had to taste his food. A week later, out of a postage stamp–sized kitchen, he produced a terrine of duck and rabbit rillettes, a leg of lamb with a gratin of courgettes and tomatoes, and a stunningly tasty grilled swordfish with braised fennel, capers, and raisins. The main course was even better: a fricassee of rabbit provençal followed by a magnificent cod dish, its lightly sautéed fillets served in a sublime white wine and garlic broth with beautifully steamed cockles.

It was almost too impressive. I was now no longer concerned that his food might not be good enough, but for a brasserie with 200 seats it might be *too* good. On a busy night at the acclaimed Daniel he'd cooked 150 dinners. At Balthazar it might be 500. Besides, Balthazar was a brasserie, not a restaurant, and would stay open twenty hours a day serving breakfast, lunch, dinner, and supper. More important, how would someone who had never yet been a chef cope with organizing and operating the kitchen of such an ambitious project? He wouldn't, Riad replied. Instead he'd share the responsibility by bringing in his partner from Daniel, Lee Hanson, as co-chef.

This wasn't what I wanted to hear. First, it meant adding another high salary to the payroll, and second, having two chefs, both equal in stature, seemed like a problem in the making. By tradition, kitchens are led—often bullied—by one chef, and one only. During the frenzied peak of a busy night, the kitchen, with its heat, steam, noise, and unstoppable rush of food orders, resembles a kind of feverish battlefield. Food is "killed," "fired," and "taken out," but on no occasion discussed. Second opinions are nonexistent. Conditions dictate that the chef is an autocrat, and that's the way it works, and has always worked, for a hundred years.

But after meeting Lee Hanson I completely changed my mind. Partly because I had no choice, but mostly because he was the first and only chef I'd ever met who seemed normal. And though I may have had questions regarding Riad's temperament under pressure, I instinctively had none with Lee. In a kitchen crisis, he seemed to be someone who would remain calm and rational. And, like Riad, he was also immensely talented.

I decided to give it a go, and from then on the three of us began meeting regularly to discuss the menu. Initially this was a bit of a tug-of-war because our restaurant experiences were so radically different. Whereas I was happy to see a menu consist of nothing but standard bistro fare, Lee and Riad understandably wanted something more challenging. I was so conscious that they were leaving a secure job with the four-star Daniel that I sometimes felt like I was luring a classically trained pianist to come join the Sex Pistols. A hamburger was the last thing they wanted on the menu! But slowly they began to warm to the egalitarian appeal of a brasserie, and slowly I began to see the folly of simply reproducing bistro food ingredient for ingredient. A sort of inspiring compromise was formed, and the closer we came to opening the more we agreed upon it. But it was always their menu, not mine. I was happy just to finish building and open the place.

Balthazar opened in the spring of 1997 and was staggeringly busy from day one. That a barely formed kitchen with a brand-new menu survived even the first week of that onslaught is a remarkable testament to Riad and Lee. Walking into that blast furnace of a kitchen on our first weekend night put into perspective how superficial my emphasis on the look and the running of the dining room had always been. Of course, those aspects of a restaurant are important, and to me probably more than they should be. But it's the kitchen, and the food that it produces, that matters most. And hopefully this will be made even clearer once you start leafing through this book.

Keith McNally

THE

BALTHAZAR

COOKBOOK

APPETIZERS, SOUPS,

POUR
COMMENCER

and BREAKFAST

BALTHAZAR SALAD

When we set out to devise a house salad that would reflect the restaurant, we decided to incorporate an ingredient for every letter in the word *Balthazar*. The Balthazar Salad was a hit, but we still don't generally recommend designing food through word-play.

SERVES 6

Trim, wash, and spin the romaine, mâche, frisée, and radicchio. Toss together in a large bowl and add the sliced fennel and sliced radishes. Set aside in the refrigerator until needed.

Prepare an ice-water bath in a large bowl and bring a pot of salted water to a boil. Cut away the woody base of the asparagus spears. With a vegetable peeler, trim the tough outer stem. Add the asparagus to the boiling water and cook for about 8 minutes, until tender. Remove with tongs to the ice bath, and add the haricots verts to the still-boiling water. Again, cook for 8 minutes, then transfer to the ice bath to refresh. Drain the asparagus and the haricots verts and add to the

lettuces along with the salt and pepper. Toss gently by hand to combine, dress with the Lemon–Truffle Vinaigrette, and toss again.

Slice the ricotta salata in ⅛-inch slices. Halve and peel the avocado and slice each half as thinly as possible. Squeeze the lemon over the slices to prevent them from discoloring.

To assemble the salad, set out 6 medium bowls. Divide the dressed lettuces and vegetables among the bowls. Top with 1 slice of ricotta salata, 2 slices of avocado, and a small bundle of julienned beet. Sprinkle with lemon zest and brioche bread crumbs.

ROASTED BEETS

Spread a bit of olive oil on a small plate. Roll each beet in the oil and wrap individually in aluminum foil along with a sprig of thyme. Bake until tender, 1 to 1½ hours, until soft and yielding when pierced with the tip of a knife. Cool, remove the skins, and slice as directed by recipe. The beets can be stored in the refrigerator, in their foil packets, until needed.

INGREDIENTS

1   head of romaine lettuce

¼   pound mâche

1   head of frisée

1   head of radicchio

1   fennel bulb, very thinly sliced, preferably on a mandoline

¼   pound radishes, thinly sliced

½   pound asparagus

¼   pound haricots verts

1   teaspoon salt

½   teaspoon freshly ground black pepper

¼   cup Lemon–Truffle Vinaigrette *(page 235)*

¼   pound ricotta salata

1   Hass avocado

1   lemon, halved

1   roasted beet *(see Note)*, julienned

    Zest of 1 lemon, blanched in boiling water for 1 minute

3   slices of brioche, toasted and then pulsed in a food processor to a fine crumb

ROASTED BEETS

AND MÂCHE SALAD

A composed salad that is light and—thanks to roasted beets and some Roquefort—substantial too. We use mâche, also known as lamb's lettuce or corn salad, for its velvety texture and clean appearance. This is a vibrant salad that looks great on the plate. Dress the components individually for just the right coverage.

SERVES 6

Preheat the oven to 375°F.

Spread the walnuts on a baking sheet and toast them in the oven for 3 to 5 minutes, or until they give off a nutty aroma. The nuts shouldn't take on any color, and they should be discarded if they turn brown.

Meanwhile, prepare an ice-water bath and bring a large pot of salted water to a boil over a high flame. Add the haricots verts and cook until tender, 5 to 10 minutes. Remove the beans using a slotted spoon or kitchen tongs, then plunge them into the ice bath. Drain and reserve. Add the sliced leeks to the still-boiling water and cook for 10 to 15 minutes, until they have lost their crunch. Remove with tongs and refresh in the ice bath. Drain and reserve.

Make the salad dressing: Combine the vinegar and the mustard in a bowl or glass measuring cup. Whisk in the grape-seed and walnut oils and season with

¼ teaspoon salt and a few grindings of pepper.

Add the cooked leeks to the chilled, diced beets. Season with salt and pepper to taste, then dress with about ¾ cup of the salad dressing. Season the haricots verts with salt to taste, and toss with about ¼ cup of the dressing.

To serve, set out 6 salad plates. On each plate, create a bed of the beet–leek mixture and top with a small bundle of haricots verts.

Make a tiny puddle of dressing in a small bowl. Divide the mâche into 6 small bouquets. Hold each bouquet by the stem end, swirl the leaves in the dressing to lightly coat, and place within the bundle of haricot verts. Arrange 2 pieces of blue cheese on each plate and top with a few toasted walnuts.

INGREDIENTS

1 cup walnuts

½ pound haricots verts

4 leeks, thinly sliced *(see page 144)*

¼ cup sherry wine vinegar

1 teaspoon Dijon mustard

¾ cup grapeseed oil or vegetable oil

¼ cup cold-pressed walnut oil

¼ teaspoon salt, plus more to taste

4 roasted medium beets *(see page 4)*, chilled and cut into ½-inch dice

Finely ground black pepper

¾ pound mâche (substitute 1 endive cut into 2-inch julienne strips, or Bibb lettuce)

¼ pound blue cheese, broken or cut into 12 pieces

CHEESE

We recommend Roquefort, France's king of blues, but for a creamier texture try a Blue Auvergne or, for a lighter alternative, a tangy goat cheese.

SALADE NIÇOISE

Along with the Caesar, the Niçoise is counted among the world's most celebrated salads. As befits its position, there are some hard-line rules regarding ingredients. This version, Niçoise in name and inspiration, contains the requisite elements along with some colorful changes, the most significant of which is the seared fresh tuna rather than the tinned type. It's a hefty salad, definitely main-course material, the only rule being that the ingredients be fresh, clean, and good-looking.

***

SERVES 6

In a medium saucepan, cover the potatoes with cold salted water and bring to a boil. Cook for 40 minutes, or until fork tender. Drain. When cool enough to handle, cut into eighths and toss with ¼ cup of the vinaigrette. Set aside.

Meanwhile, prepare an ice-water bath and bring another medium saucepan of salted water to a boil. Add the haricots verts and cook for about 8 minutes, until tender (we're opposed to crunch in a cooked vegetable). Strain and plunge into the ice bath so they retain their color. Strain, dry with paper towels, and set aside.

Season the tuna on both sides with ½ teaspoon of salt and ¼ teaspoon of pepper. Heat the olive oil in a large nonstick skillet over a high flame until it begins to smoke. Sear the tuna for 2 minutes on each side for rare, or continue cooking, up to 4 minutes per side, for tuna that is well done. Cut across the grain into ½-inch slices.

In a large bowl, toss the arugula, bell peppers, onion, radishes, tomatoes, cucumbers, and the reserved haricots verts with the remaining dressing; everything should be evenly coated. Add the already dressed potatoes, and gently toss with additional salt and freshly ground pepper to taste.

Divide the salad among 6 individual bowls. Garnish the top of each with a few slices of tuna, 4 hard-boiled egg wedges, 4 olives, and 2 anchovy fillets. Serve soon after plating.

INGREDIENTS

4 Yukon gold potatoes, about 1¼ pounds

¾ cup Balsamic Vinaigrette *(page 237)*

6 ounces haricots verts

1 pound top-quality tuna, cut into 2-inch-thick steaks

½ teaspoon salt, plus more to taste

¼ teaspoon freshly ground black pepper, plus more to taste

3 tablespoons olive oil

¾ pound arugula, stemmed, washed, and spun dry

1 red bell pepper, cored and cut into thin strips

1 yellow bell pepper, cored and cut into thin strips

1 red onion, halved and cut into ⅛-inch-wide slices

6 radishes, thinly sliced

9 red cherry tomatoes, halved

9 yellow cherry tomatoes, halved

1 cucumber, peeled, halved lengthwise, seeds removed, and sliced

6 hard-boiled eggs *(page 24)*, cut into quarters

24 Niçoise olives

12 anchovy fillets

FRISÉE AUX LARDONS

This classic salad is dressed with a vinaigrette made from olive oil and warm bacon fat. Along with the bitter greens and salty bacon, the runny yolk of a poached egg flows down onto the other ingredients and serves as a rich sauce. This is a lunch unto itself, a filling late-night supper, or a first course for those who believe strongly in bacon fat.

SERVES 6

INGREDIENTS

6 slices of stale brioche

4 heads of frisée, cored, rinsed, spun dry, and torn into bite-size pieces

1 tablespoon plus ½ cup sherry vinegar

½ pound slab bacon, cut into ½-inch lardons

4 shallots, peeled and minced (about ½ cup)

½ cup olive oil

½ teaspoon salt, plus more to taste

¼ teaspoon freshly ground black pepper, plus more to taste

3 tablespoons fines herbes (*page 87*)

6 large eggs
Sea salt

Preheat the oven to 375°F.

Trim the crusts from the bread and cut into ½-inch cubes. Place on a sheet tray and bake in the oven until golden brown, about 10 minutes. Shake the pan halfway through to toast evenly. Combine the croutons in a large bowl with the clean frisée.

Prepare the pan for poaching the eggs: Fill a wide, straight-sided sauté pan with water (about two-thirds full) and add the tablespoon of vinegar. Over a medium-high flame, bring to a gentle simmer, and adjust the heat to maintain it.

In a dry skillet or sauté pan over medium heat, brown the lardons well on all sides, about 10 minutes. Add the minced shallots and continue to cook for 2 to 3 minutes, to soften and lightly brown them. Without pouring off the fat, add the ½ cup of vinegar to the pan. Bring to a boil, using a wooden spoon to scrape any delicious bits that have caramelized on the surface of the pan. When the vinegar has reduced by half, about 3 minutes, turn off the flame. Add the olive oil, salt, and pepper, and stir well to combine. Pour this warm vinaigrette with bacon into the bowl of frisée, along with the croutons and fines herbes. Toss well to combine. Divide the salad among 6 serving plates, piled in small heaps.

Crack the eggs, one at a time, into a small saucer and then slide them into the simmering water. Poach for 4 minutes, resulting in a set white and a cooked but runny yolk. With a slotted spoon, scoop out the poached eggs, one at a time, drain, and position on top of each pile of frisée. Sprinkle with crunchy sea salt and a few turns of a peppermill. Serve immediately.

LARDONS

Lardons, or nice-sized (about ½-inch) cubes of bacon, should be cut from a slab from which the rind has been removed.

CHICKEN LIVER MOUSSE

At the restaurant this mousse is flavored with foie gras. But here we offer a streamlined version using only chicken liver. With or without the deluxe inclusion, it's a fine plated appetizer or hors d'oeuvre.

SERVES 6

Preheat the oven to 300°F.

Using 4 tablespoons of melted butter and a pastry brush, thoroughly coat the inside of six 4-ounce ramekins.

Place the chicken livers in a blender. Add the egg, salt, quatre-épices powder, white pepper, and Cognac. Process until smoothly combined, about 20 seconds. With the blender still running, add the remaining ½ pound of melted butter and continue blending for 15 seconds.

Pour the mousse mixture into the prepared ramekins until three-fourths full. Place the ramekins in a baking dish and fill the dish with warm water to half the height of the ramekins. Carefully transfer to the oven and bake for 30 minutes, or until the mousse is firm to the touch.

Let the ramekins cool, and then refrigerate until needed. Run a warm knife around the inner edge of each ramekin, cover with a plate, and then invert. Serve chilled with baguette toasts.

FOIE GRAS MOUSSE

It's difficult to buy a small amount of foie gras—the liver is generally sold in whole lobes costing around fifty dollars. A few tablespoons of store-bought foie gras mousse—about 3 ounces—can provide the suggestion of that lush flavor without the expense. Add this mousse to the livers and other ingredients prior to combining them in a blender.

QUATRE-ÉPICES

Quatre-épices, or four-spice powder, is a blend of nutmeg, cloves, cinnamon, and allspice, used most often to flavor terrines. Make your own in a spice grinder or buy it pre-packaged.

INGREDIENTS

½ pound (2 sticks) plus
   4 tablespoons unsalted
   butter, melted

1 pound chicken livers

1 large egg

2 teaspoons salt

Pinch of quatre-épices
(see Note)

Pinch of freshly ground
white pepper

2 tablespoons Cognac

1 baguette, sliced and toasted,
for serving

RILLETTES À LA FERMIÈRE

Rillettes—pork, duck, and rabbit cooked, shredded, and stored in a crock of fat—is a staple of French life, and a wonderful addition to an American one. Our authentic rillettes are packed into a terrine, but you could just as easily store and serve this recipe in the more traditional glass jars or earthenware pots. We add dried fruits for a hint of sweetness in the midst of all that fatty richness. Serve with toasted rustic bread and some cornichons.

MAKES 1½ QUARTS, SERVES 10

PHOTOGRAPH BY CHRISTOPHER HIRSHEIMER

INGREDIENTS

2 tablespoons sugar

2 teaspoons quatre-épices *(see page 12)*

1 teaspoon freshly ground white pepper

1 whole rabbit, cut into 6 pieces

2 Moulard duck legs (about 2 pounds)

1 pound pork butt, cut into 4 chunks

½ cup coarse sea salt

2 heads of garlic, the cloves of 1 peeled and smashed, the other halved horizontally

2 cinnamon sticks

½ teaspoon juniper berries

4 whole cloves

4 star anise pods

1 teaspoon black peppercorns

2 quarts duck fat (available from D'Artagnan, 1-800-DAR-TAGN or www.dartagnan.com)

½ cup dried fruits (cherries, prunes, apricots), quartered

½ cup brandy or Armagnac

Cure the meats: In a small bowl, combine the sugar, quartre-épices, and white pepper. Rub the rabbit, duck, and pork with the seasoning mixture and arrange in a large bowl or enameled pot. Add the salt, smashed garlic, cinnamon, juniper, cloves, star anise, and peppercorns. Cover and refrigerate for 24 hours.

The next day preheat the oven to 300°F.

Render the duck fat in a large Dutch oven over a medium-low flame. Remove the meats from the salt mixture, reserving the spices. Brush lightly to remove excess seasoning and add to the duck fat. Wrap the spices and the halved head of garlic in cheesecloth, tie with kitchen twine, and add the sachet to the pot. Bring to a gentle simmer. Cover with a tight-fitting lid and transfer to the preheated oven. Cook for 3 hours, or until the meats are falling off their bones.

Meanwhile, soak the dried fruits in the brandy until needed.

When the meat is finished cooking, use tongs to remove the meat from the duck fat and set aside in a large bowl until cool enough to handle. Remove 2 cups of duck fat from the pot and set aside.

Pull all the meat from the bones, discarding the skin, fat, and bones. Shred the meat and place in a large bowl. Begin adding the reserved duck fat and stir with a wooden spoon to incorporate. When all the duck fat has been added, drain the macerated fruit and stir to combine.

Fill a Pyrex loaf pan or a terrine with the rillettes, taking care to distribute the fruit evenly throughout. Cut a piece of parchment paper or wax paper to the size of the terrine and cover. Wait at least 24 hours before serving, but 1 week would be better. To serve, run a warm blade around the edge of the terrine and then invert onto a cutting board or durable platter. Cut 1-inch slices and serve with grilled country bread and cornichons.

BRANDADE DE MORUE

Brandade was first made in Languedoc, in southwestern France, where salt cod (salted and dried preserved cod) was pummeled and enriched with olive oil, garlic, and milk. In the early nineteenth century the dish made its way north to become a mainstay in both Paris restaurants and the mess halls of the French army. Potatoes were added to cut the taste as well as the cost of the fish, and they are now indispensable, no matter what the cook's budget. Serve as an appetizer or hors d'oeuvre. Reconstitute salt cod by soaking overnight with three changes of water.

SERVES 6

In a small saucepan, heat the olive oil and the rosemary, thyme, and sage over a low flame for 3 minutes, allowing the herbs to infuse the oil. Discard the herbs and set the oil aside.

Combine the garlic and cream in a small saucepan over a medium flame. Bring to a boil, turn the heat down to a simmer, and cook for 15 to 30 minutes, or until the garlic is very soft. Pour the mixture into a blender and purée. Keep a firm grip on the lid, as the heat from the cream mixture will force the lid up. Set aside, with the intention of reheating it later in either a saucepan or in a microwave. (The garlic-infused cream can be prepared a day in advance and stored, covered, in the refrigerator.)

Drain the cod, trim away any dark pieces of flesh, and cut the fish into 2-inch chunks. Place in a 5-quart saucepan with the potatoes and water to cover. Bring to a boil, then reduce the heat to low and simmer for 30 minutes, or until the potatoes are tender and the fish flaky. Drain in a colander.

Transfer the fish–potato mixture to the bowl of a standing mixer. Using the paddle attachment, process for 30 seconds. Drizzle in the reserved herb-infused olive oil, and then two thirds of the reserved garlic cream. After the cream has been incorporated, continue mixing for 30 seconds.

Serve from a communal bowl or on individual plates. Drizzle the remaining third of the garlic cream over the brandade and serve with toasted baguette slices.

INGREDIENTS

¼ cup olive oil

1 sprig of rosemary

3 sprigs of thyme

2 sage leaves

10 garlic cloves, peeled and cut in thirds

1½ cups heavy cream

1 pound salt cod, soaked overnight in a large bowl of water, changed three times

3 large Idaho potatoes (about 1¾ pounds), peeled and cut into sixths

1 baguette, thinly sliced, brushed with olive oil, and either toasted or browned in a frying pan

QUENELLES DE POISSON

This airy fish mousse is shaped into a classic dumpling form from which quenelles get their name (from the German *Knödel*). These come together quickly with just a few minutes of poaching time and are served as an appetizer with Sauce Américaine. Make sure all the ingredients are cold before mixing. Garnish the dish with the lobster meat left over from the Sauce Américaine preparation.

MAKES 24 QUENELLES

Place the scallops and cod in the work bowl of a food processor. Pulse for 5 seconds, and then add the salt, pepper, and the egg whites. Process for 10 seconds and then drizzle the cream through the feed tube while the machine is running, about 30 seconds total, until a mousse forms. Refrigerate for at least 30 minutes or overnight.

Bring a small saucepan of lightly salted water to a simmer. Have two soup spoons (oval, not rounded) at the ready. Dip the spoons into the water and then scoop a spoonful of mousse. Form a quenelle by holding the other spoon over the mound

and using it to smooth the mousse into an egg shape, rolling it from one spoon to the other to achieve a defined and firm shape. When the quenelle is formed, dip the empty spoon into the simmering water. Scoop the quenelle onto the warm wet spoon and then slide it smoothly into the water. Poach for 7 minutes, turning halfway through.

Continue with the remaining mousse. Remove the cooked quenelles with a slotted spoon and serve immediately with Sauce Américaine, or cool on a paper towel and then refrigerate to reheat in the sauce.

INGREDIENTS

½ pound sea scallops
½ pound cod fillet, cut into 2-inch chunks
½ teaspoon salt

¼ teaspoon freshly ground white pepper
3 egg whites
1 cup heavy cream
Sauce Américaine *(page 246)*

ESCARGOTS

WITH GARLIC BUTTER

Waiter, there's a snail on my plate.

SERVES 6

Preheat the broiler.

Combine the softened butter with the garlic, parsley, chives, basil, thyme, lemon juice, salt, and pepper. This can be done with a standing electric mixer using the paddle attachment, or by hand with a wooden spoon. After the herbs are thoroughly combined, chill the compound butter until needed.

Bring the Court Bouillon or water to a boil and add the snails. Reduce the heat to a simmer and cook for 8 minutes. Drain. The snails can now be either tucked into a shell or set into escargot dishes, or put into a medium gratin dish. Top each snail with a tablespoon-size scoop of the herb butter. If using shells, set them into an ovenproof casserole or baking dish. Slide the escargot dishes or the gratin dish into the broiler for 5 to 8 minutes, until the butter is bubbling hot. Serve straight from the broiler with a good crusty bread so as not to miss one drop of the garlic butter.

INGREDIENTS

1 pound (4 sticks) unsalted butter, softened to room temperature

8 garlic cloves, finely chopped (¼ cup)

½ cup chopped flat-leaf parsley

¼ cup chopped chives

¼ cup chopped basil

2 tablespoons chopped thyme

2 tablespoons fresh lemon juice

1 teaspoon kosher salt

½ teaspoon freshly ground black pepper

1 quart Court Bouillon *(page 234)* or water

1 pound escargots, canned, rinsed thoroughly *(see page 20)*

SNAILS

As with French wine, cheese, or lingerie, snails are the subject of national organizations, secret night markets, and spirited discussion. And like wine lovers, the escargot eaters of France cite favorite regions (the snail is the official emblem of Burgundy) along with seasonal preferences (the rainy summer producing a more succulent snail with higher moisture content).

The U.S. market for snails takes a more one-size-fits-all approach. Farmed snails are widely sold in cans with their accompanying shells included, as are imported French snails. Canned snails are already cooked and require only a reheating in either boiling water or the more flavorful Court Bouillon (page 234); they're widely available and extremely convenient.

If fresh live snails are available, prepare them for cooking in the following manner: In a shallow baking dish or pan, soak the snails in lukewarm water for 10 minutes. Discard any snails that haven't begun to emerge from their shells. Moisten the rim of a large bowl and then press the rim onto a plate of salt to coat. Place the snails in the bowl and cover with water and 1 teaspoon of salt. The snails will emerge from their shells. Proceed with cooking the snails in Court Bouillon as directed by the recipe.

GRAVLAX

Taking the traditional gravlax process a step further, we follow the salt-curing process by marinating the salmon in olive oil and toasted spices. The moisture removed by salt-curing is replaced with the flavor-infused oil, giving the salmon a pronounced silky texture. This method, which should take place over five days, is centuries old. The only difference today is that instead of salting and burying the salmon in the cold Scandinavian ground as the Norwegians did, we now opt for the back of a cold Sub-Zero. Serve with brown bread and a mustard sauce to enhance this light and refreshing appetizer.

SERVES 6

DAY 1

Use a very sharp knife to score the salmon's skin, making slashes about 3 inches long and ⅛ inch deep. Place in a small casserole dish, not much larger than the fillet itself and add the vodka.

Combine the salt and sugar in a bowl. Rub a handful of the salt mixture onto the fillet and then spread half of the remaining salt mixture in the bottom of the casserole dish. Place the fillet, skin side down, in the dish and cover with 1 clove of garlic, the zest of 1 lemon, 3 sprigs of parsley, 3 sprigs of thyme, 3 sprigs of dill, and the remaining salt mixture. Cover with plastic and refrigerate for 48 hours.

DAY 2

Meet friends for lunch, followed by dinner in a large, bustling brasserie.

DAY 3

Preheat the oven to 350°F. Spread the coriander seeds, fennel seeds, black peppercorns, star anise, and mustard seeds on a cookie sheet or in an ovenproof sauté pan. Toast in the oven for about 5 minutes, or until the spices give off a fragrant aroma.

Remove the salmon from the fridge and rinse under cold water to remove the salt and spices; rinse the dish clean as well. Put the salmon back into the clean dish along with the remaining sliced garlic, lemon zest, and herb sprigs. Add the olive oil and the toasted coriander, fennel, peppercorns, star anise, and mustard. Cover with plastic wrap and marinate for at least 48 hours or up to 10 days.

DAY 4

Sleep through morning appointments; wake up around 2:45 P.M. for lunch in a large, bustling brasserie.

DAY 5

To serve, thinly slice the fish on a bias, starting at the tail end. Serve with Mustard Sauce. Besides brown bread, Gravlox is excellent with blini or potato pancakes.

INGREDIENTS

1½ pounds salmon fillet, skin on

¼ cup vodka

2 cups kosher salt

1 cup sugar

2 garlic cloves, thinly sliced

3 lemons, zested

8 sprigs of flat-leaf parsley

8 sprigs of thyme

11 sprigs of dill

1 tablespoon coriander seeds

1 tablespoon fennel seeds

1 tablespoon whole black peppercorns

2 star anise pods

1 tablespoon mustard seeds

2 cups olive oil

Mustard Sauce *(recipe follows)*

MUSTARD SAUCE

MAKES 1 CUP

Juice of 1 lemon

1 tablespoon dark brown sugar

3 tablespoons Dijon mustard

⅓ cup grapeseed oil

1 tablespoon chopped dill

Combine the lemon juice, sugar, and mustard in a small bowl. Gradually whisk in the grapeseed oil to create an emulsion, and then add the chopped dill. Chill before serving.

GRILLED SARDINE PAN BAGNAT

At Balthazar the *pan bagnat,* or "bathed bread," is served open face and eaten with a fork. Presented as an assemblage of cool, crisp vegetables and fresh sardines with excellent bread from our bakery, it's as near to elegant as a sardine sandwich can get.

SERVES 6

Prepare an ice-water bath and bring a medium saucepan of salted water to a boil. Add the string beans and cook for 5 to 7 minutes, or until tender. With a slotted spoon or tongs, transfer to the ice bath. Drain and set aside.

In a large bowl, whisk ½ cup olive oil and the balsamic vinegar together. Add the blanched string beans, fennel, roasted peppers, and cherry tomatoes. Add ½ teaspoon salt, ¼ teaspoon freshly ground pepper, and ¼ cup fresh basil. Toss to thoroughly coat the vegetables. Do this in advance (but don't refrigerate) as the vegetables are all the better for it.

Brush the sardines generously with olive oil and season with ½ teaspoon salt and

¼ teaspoon freshly ground black pepper. Grill over medium heat or broil for 2 to 3 minutes.

Drizzle the slices of bread with olive oil (hold your thumb over the top of the bottle while pouring) and grill or toast. Spread a bit of Tapenade on each slice. Place the toasts on small plates, layer a few leaves of arugula on each slice, and then top with a full assortment of marinated vegetables, 3 grilled sardines, and a couple of slices of hard-boiled egg. Drizzle the pan bagnats with any remaining dressing and garnish with olives. Serve as an appetizer or light lunch.

HARD-BOILED EGGS

Bring a medium saucepan of water to a boil, then lower the flame to a soft simmer. Use a slotted spoon to lower each egg gently to the bottom (be sure not to crowd the pan). Cook for 7 minutes for a yolk that's firm but still slightly creamy. Remove the eggs with the slotted spoon, let cool to room temperature, and serve or refrigerate. Don't peel until just before using.

INGREDIENTS

¼ pound string beans or haricots verts

½ cup extra-virgin olive oil, plus additional for brushing the sardines and drizzling

3 tablespoons balsamic vinegar

1 fennel bulb, washed and cut into thin matchsticks

1 roasted red bell pepper *(see page 249)*, cut into matchsticks

1 roasted yellow bell pepper *(see page 249)*, cut into matchsticks

½ pound cherry tomatoes, halved

1 teaspoon salt

½ teaspoon freshly ground black pepper

1 bunch of fresh basil, chopped

18 fresh sardines, cleaned and filleted

6 slices of hearty country bread

2 to 3 tablespoons Tapenade *(olive paste, page 238)*

1 bunch of arugula, washed well and spun dry

3 hard-boiled eggs *(see Note)*

½ pound Niçoise olives

— 25 —

STEAK TARTARE

We prefer to mix our Steak Tartare in the kitchen rather than the more crowd-pleasing tableside preparation. Not because we don't trust our waiters (although we don't), but because we want to ensure consistency. The beef is hand-chopped, mixed with a fork, and then sent off to the table. The bowl it was mixed in then gets passed to one of our line cooks. He'll add a little chopped jalapeño (he always keeps a pepper in his chef coat) and, like chocolate frosting and a finger, will scrape the bowl clean with a crouton.

SERVES 6 TO 8

Remove the beef from the refrigerator; it should be very cold. Using a very sharp chef's knife, cut the steak into thin ¼-inch slices. Stack 3 of the slices and slice lengthwise, every ½ inch, holding the stack in place. Then cut across the stack, again every ½ inch, cutting the steak into ½-inch dice. Hold the chopped steak in a bowl set over crushed ice in a larger bowl.

When all of the beef has been chopped, add the onion, capers, cornichons, parsley, anchovy, oil, garlic, salt, and pepper. Gently mix with a fork until just combined. Add the Tartare Mayonnaise and again mix gently until just combined.

Serve on individual plates with baguette slices alongside.

INGREDIENTS

1¼ pounds filet mignon, very cold

½ medium onion, minced

2 tablespoons capers

8 cornichons, cut into small dice

2 tablespoons flat-leaf parsley, chopped

1 anchovy fillet, minced

2 tablespoons extra-virgin olive oil

1 garlic clove, peeled and minced

½ teaspoon salt

White pepper

6 tablespoons Tartare Mayonnaise *(see page 250)*

1 baguette, sliced

STEAK FOR TARTARE

Buy top-quality steak from the best butcher you know. Prepare the tartare just before eating and place the serving bowl in a larger bowl of ice to keep it cold.

GOAT CHEESE TART

WITH CARAMELIZED ONIONS

This tart benefits from a brief rest when it comes out of the oven; the flavor is best when it's warm, not hot. A heap of simply dressed cherry tomatoes looks bright alongside, and a dollop of Tapenade *(page 238)* adds some kick. Be sure to buy fresh, not aged, goat cheese. This recipe makes one 10-inch or six 4-inch tarts. In either case, use fluted tart pans with removable bottoms.

SERVES 6

To make the crusts, combine the flour, salt, and chilled butter in the bowl of a food processor. Pulse until the mixture looks like coarse meal, about 10 seconds. With the machine running, add the 2 egg yolks and ice water through the feed tube. Continue to process until the dough forms a ball, about 20 seconds. With lightly floured hands, shape the dough into 1 disk if making the 10-inch tart, or into 6 equally sized disks if making the 4-inch tarts. Wrap in plastic and refrigerate for at least 1 hour, or overnight.

Preheat oven to 350°F. Remove the dough from the refrigerator.

Over a low flame, heat the olive oil in a large skillet. Add the onions, thyme, bay leaf, and ½ teaspoon each of salt and pepper. Stir occasionally, cooking the onions until soft and golden, reducing their volume by nearly half; this can take up to 1 hour. Remove from the pan with a slotted spoon, draining off any excess oil. Discard the thyme and bay leaf.

Meanwhile, roll out the dough on a lightly floured surface to ⅛-inch thickness. Coat the tart pan(s) with nonstick spray. Fit the dough snugly into the pan, pressing it firmly into the bottom edge and fluted sides. Trim the excess with a sharp knife, and prick the dough several times with the tines of a fork. Place the tart pan on a sheet tray for easy handling. Line the dough with aluminum foil, and weigh down with raw rice or beans. Bake for 15 minutes. Remove the foil and weights and continue to bake a few minutes more, until the crust takes on a light brown color. Remove from the oven and allow to cool while the filling is completed.

In a food processor or in the bowl of an electric mixer, mix the goat cheese, cream cheese, 2 eggs, and the remaining ½ teaspoon each of salt and pepper. Process until smooth.

Spread the caramelized onions evenly over the bottom of the prebaked tart shell and pour the cheese mixture over the onions, filling to just below the rim. Using a wide pastry brush, gently brush the beaten egg yolk over the top of the tart. Aim for complete coverage.

Bake for 12 minutes, until set. Allow to cool for 15 minutes and serve warm.

INGREDIENTS

FOR THE CRUST

1¾ cups all-purpose flour

1 teaspoon salt

1 stick plus 2 tablespoons cold, unsalted butter, cut into 10 pieces

2 extra-large egg yolks

3 tablespoons ice-cold water

FOR THE FILLING

¼ cup olive oil

3 large yellow onions, halved through the stem end and thinly sliced into ⅛-inch half-moons

1 sprig of thyme

1 bay leaf

1 teaspoon salt

1 teaspoon freshly ground black pepper

8 ounces fresh goat cheese, at room temperature

8 ounces cream cheese, at room temperature

2 extra-large eggs

1 extra-large egg yolk, beaten

POTAGE SAINT-GERMAIN

Saint-Germain is the culinary term for a preparation using green peas or a pea purée. This thick soup uses split peas, which can be enjoyed year-round.

Cut the brioche into 1-inch-square croutons. Melt the butter in a sauté pan over medium heat. When the foam subsides, add the croutons and toast until golden brown. Put the croutons in a resealable plastic bag with ½ teaspoon of the salt, ¼ teaspoon black pepper, and the chopped rosemary. Gently shake to season the croutons and then set aside until needed.

Set a stockpot over a medium flame and add the bacon. Cook for 3 to 5 minutes, stirring occasionally as the bacon browns and renders fat into the pot. Add the olive oil and the diced carrot, onion, and celery.

Stir thoroughly to coat the vegetables and cook for 8 minutes, until the vegetables are soft but not brown. Add the split peas, bouquet garni, and 1 teaspoon of the salt. Stir well and cook for 5 minutes. Add the Chicken Stock, bring to a boil over high heat, then reduce to a simmer. Cook for 1 hour, or until the peas are soft and yielding.

Remove and discard the bouquet garni and the bacon. With an immersion blender or regular blender, purée to a full-bodied smoothness. Taste to correct the seasoning. Serve hot with the reserved croutons.

INGREDIENTS

- 6 slices of brioche or white bread
- 3 tablespoons unsalted butter
- 1½ teaspoons salt, plus more to taste
- ¼ teaspoon freshly ground black pepper, plus more to taste
- 1 teaspoon chopped fresh rosemary
- ¼ pound smoked slab bacon

- 2 tablespoons olive oil
- 1 large carrot, diced small
- ½ medium yellow onion, diced small
- 2 celery stalks, diced small
- 1 pound split peas
- 1 bouquet garni (see Note)
- 2 quarts Chicken Stock (page 230)

BOUQUET GARNI

A bundle of herbs that's either tied together with a string or wrapped in cheesecloth to form a sachet. We use 6 to 8 sprigs of parsley, 3 sprigs of thyme, and a bay leaf.

MUSHROOM SOUP

This hearty purée combines velvety fresh mushrooms with the concentrated intensity of dried ones. The result is a deeply flavored soup that's ready to eat in under an hour. Clean the fresh mushrooms with a damp paper towel or scrape them clean with a paring knife. Choose mushrooms that are firm and moist but not soggy. They should be in good form, indicating that they've been carefully handled.

SERVES 6

Soak the dry mushrooms in 1 cup of warm water for 20 to 30 minutes, until plump. Strain the soaking liquid through a coffee filter to remove grit and reserve, along with the reconstituted mushrooms, until needed.

Heat the olive oil in a large pot over a medium flame. Bundle the rosemary and sage together and tie with kitchen twine. When the oil is hot, add the herb bundle and sizzle for a few minutes on both sides to infuse the oil.

Add the onion, garlic, salt, and pepper and cook for 5 minutes, until the onion is soft and translucent but not brown. Turn the flame to high and add the white mushrooms and shiitakes. Cook for 10 minutes, during which the mushrooms will give off their liquid (which should evaporate quickly due to the high heat) and deflate significantly. Stir occasionally.

Add the Chicken Stock and the dried mushrooms along with the soaking water. Simmer for 30 minutes. Remove the herbs, then add the cream and butter. Working in batches, purée the soup in a blender until smooth. Return to the pot and keep at a very low simmer until ready to serve.

INGREDIENTS

1 ounce dry mushrooms (porcini, morels, or shiitakes)

½ cup olive oil

2 sprigs of rosemary

4 sprigs of sage

1 large yellow onion, peeled and thinly sliced

3 garlic cloves, peeled and thinly sliced

1½ teaspoons salt

¼ teaspoon freshly ground white pepper

1 pound white button mushrooms, cleaned and thinly sliced

1 pound shiitake mushrooms, stemmed, cleaned, and thinly sliced

6 cups Chicken Stock (*page 230*) or water

1 cup heavy cream

2 tablespoons unsalted butter

OEUFS EN MEURETTE

Brunch at Balthazar attracts a huge and varied following of locals, out-of-towners, chefs on their day off, and even a priest or two cutting class. With over a thousand dishes cooked in six hours, the kitchen is a complete madhouse gone haywire. But for the customer, it's a day of indulgence that, hopefully, involves a little too much rich food, an extra Bloody Mary, and an off-limits chocolate dessert followed by the kind of Sunday nap that almost puts off Monday morning forever.

For those who have that luxury, there's perhaps no better meal than Oeufs en Meurette—eggs poached in red wine. While it has all the components of a traditional American breakfast (bacon, eggs, and toast), it also makes a substantial supper.

SERVES 4

Set a medium saucepan of water over a high flame. When it reaches a boil, add the onions and blanch for 8 minutes until tender. Drain and set aside.

Meanwhile, brown the lardons in a small, dry sauté pan, about 10 minutes. Remove with a slotted spoon, reserve, and pour off all but 2 tablespoons of the rendered fat. Add the drained pearl onions to the pan over a high flame and sauté until they take on color, about 5 minutes. Add the mushrooms and sauté for 5 minutes, until they and the onions are golden brown. Drain whatever fat is left in the pan, and add the Sauce Bordelaise and the lardons. Bring to a slow simmer. (If not using the Sauce Bordelaise, combine the onions, mushrooms, and lardons in the pan. Keep warm over a low flame, adding butter to the pan if it dries.)

In a small skillet, bring the red wine to a simmer over medium heat. Remove the eggs from the refrigerator (they should be cold before poaching) and crack 2 into a small saucer. Slowly slip the eggs into the simmering wine and poach until the yolks are just set but still runny, about 5 minutes. Cook 4 eggs at a time. While the eggs cook, place one piece of toast in each of 4 shallow bowls. When the eggs are done, use a slotted spoon to transfer them to the toast, 2 eggs per bowl. Cover while the remaining eggs are poached.

When all the eggs are cooked and sitting on toast, season with the salt and pepper. Top with the simmering Sauce Bordelaise, and spoon the lardons and mushrooms over the top. Garnish with a little frisée alongside.

INGREDIENTS

½ cup peeled pearl onions

½ pound slab bacon, sliced into ½-inch lardons

½ pound small white button mushrooms, stems discarded (or medium-sized, stems discarded and caps sliced)

1 cup Sauce Bordelaise *(page 248)*, optional but highly recommended

1 bottle full-bodied red wine (such as a cabernet sauvignon)

8 large eggs, cold from the refrigerator

4 thick slices of country bread, crusts removed and toasted

½ teaspoon salt

¼ teaspoon freshly ground black pepper

1 bunch of frisée

ONION SOUP GRATINÉE

This simple and hearty soup, rich with burnished onions and sweet port, is topped with tangy Gruyère. Borrow a custom from Bordeaux and spill a little red wine into the bottom of your nearly empty soup bowl. The tradition, known as *chabrot*, dictates a quick swirl of wine into the tail-end of the hot broth and then a hearty gulp right from the bowl. Tradition does not dictate doing all of this while undressed, but rumor has it that it makes the soup taste even better. We've been too shy to try it.

SERVES 6

In a 5-quart Dutch oven or other large, heavy pot, heat the olive oil over a medium flame. Add the onions and, stirring frequently to prevent burning, sauté until they reach a golden color, approximately 30 minutes. Add the butter, garlic, thyme, bay leaf, salt, and pepper and cook for 10 minutes. Raise the heat to high, add the white wine, bring to a boil, and reduce the wine by half, about 3 to 5 minutes. Add the Chicken Stock and simmer for 45 minutes.

Preheat the broiler.

Remove the thyme sprigs and bay leaf, and swirl the port into the finished soup. Ladle the soup into 6 ovenproof bowls. Fit the toasted bread into the bowls on top of the liquid, and sprinkle ⅓ cup of Gruyère onto each slice. Place under the broiler for 3 minutes, or until the cheese melts to a crispy golden brown. Allow the soup to cool slightly, about 3 minutes, before serving.

INGREDIENTS

¼ cup plus 1 tablespoon olive oil

4 medium yellow onions, peeled, halved through the stem end, and sliced ¼-inch thick

1 tablespoon unsalted butter

1 garlic clove, peeled and thinly sliced

4 sprigs of thyme

1 bay leaf

1 teaspoon salt

¼ teaspoon freshly ground white pepper

¾ cup dry white wine

2 quarts Chicken Stock *(page 230)*

½ cup port

6 slices of country bread, about 1 inch thick, toasted

2 cups Gruyère cheese, coarsely grated

PLATEAU DES FRUITS DE MER

The Balthazar Platter is a towering three-tiered cascade of cooked and raw seafood, served gleaming and fresh over ice. This dramatic presentation is a Paris tradition dating back to French aristocrats of the seventeenth century who were devoted to excess in all areas. Based on the popularity of the Plateau des Fruits de Mer, excess still has a following.

Along with shellfish poached in Court Bouillon *(page 234)*, oysters are the focal point. Purchase them only on the day you intend to eat them, then store them on ice, in the refrigerator.

Shucking an oyster is a simple task: With a shucking blade (sold at all kitchenware stores), hold the oyster flat on a table or cutting board. Hold a kitchen towel over the oyster with one hand. At the hinge end of the oyster, look for a small crack or opening, or a small spot where the seal isn't tight. With your knife hand, slide the blade in, as close to the hinge as possible. Put weight on the blade, pressing down, so the top shell of the oyster is gently forced open. Remove the top shell and run the blade under the oyster to free it from the bottom shell. Serve over crushed ice and with the three sauces on page 41. Shuck the oysters just minutes before serving, and keep them very cold.

OYSTERS

BELON: From the Brittany coast of France, these have a round, flat shell and a pronounced mineral quality.

BLUE POINTS: Farmed off Long Island, New York, blue points are clean-tasting and juicy.

FANNY BAY: From British Columbia, these are sweet, plump, and firm with a saline quality.

HOOD CANAL: From the Puget Sound in Washington State, hoods are sweet and delicious, with a wonderful brininess.

KUMAMOTO: Now cultivated in Washington State, these have a buttery rich flavor with a firm, tight texture. An excellent "beginner" oyster.

MALAPEQUES: From Prince Edward Island, Canada, these are sweet, small, and thin.

QUILCENE BAY: A delicate flavor and texture are the earmarks of these Washington State oysters.

SKOOKUM: Also from the Puget Sound, these are exceptionally sweet with an almost fruity finish.

WELLFLEET: Harvested in Cape Cod, Wellfleets are small to medium with a flat oval shell, and a mild saline quality that finishes cleanly.

SHELLFISH COOKED IN COURT BOUILLON

Prepare an ice-water bath in a large bowl and set a stockpot of Court Bouillon *(page 234)* over a high flame. Once it reaches a boil, add any of the following:

PRAWNS, HEADS ON

Add up to 3 pounds of medium prawns (10 per pound) at once. Cook for 5 minutes and then use a large slotted spoon to transfer them to the ice bath. Cool for 3 minutes before peeling, leaving the heads on if desired.

LIVE LOBSTERS

Add 2 live lobsters at a time (1¼ pounds each). Cook for 7 minutes, remove with tongs, and cover with ice to cool. Split the tails using a sharp knife, and use shellfish crackers or a knife to split the claws. *(See page 247 for tips on removing the meat.)*

JONAH CRABS

Add up to 3 crabs at a time. Cook for 15 minutes and then use tongs to transfer the crabs to the ice bath. Peel the top shell by hand, and then split the body down the middle with a sharp knife. Use shellfish crackers on the claws.

COCKTAIL SAUCE
MAKES ¾ CUP

½ cup ketchup
1 tablespoon Worcestershire sauce
½ teaspoon Tabasco sauce
1 tablespoon brandy
1 teaspoon red wine vinegar
Juice of 1 lemon
2 teaspoons prepared horseradish
½ teaspoon salt

Mix all ingredients and stir to thoroughly combine. Serve cold.

MIGNONETTE SAUCE
MAKES 1 CUP

Named for the sachets of peppercorns that used to flavor soups, this has the requisite peppery bite.

½ cup red wine vinegar
½ cup sherry vinegar
2 shallots, finely chopped
1 tablespoon coarsely ground black pepper
½ teaspoon salt

Whisk all ingredients together. Serve at room temperature.

TARRAGON MAYONNAISE
MAKES ¾ CUP

½ cup Mayonnaise *(page 250)*
2 tablespoons finely chopped fresh tarragon
2 tablespoons ketchup
½ teaspoon Tabasco sauce
Pinch of cayenne pepper
2 teaspoons brandy
1 teaspoon fresh lemon juice (from about ¼ lemon)

Stir all ingredients together until smooth. Refrigerate and serve cold.

FISH

LES POISSONS

and SHELLFISH

BOUILLABAISSE

Bouillabaisse provokes strong opinions. While the mayor of Cassis felt that adding white wine was culinary heresy, the less exalted—but just as passionate—felt otherwise. The same controversy over ingredients persists today, with one school of thought insisting that saffron is imperative, while another claims that without scorpion fish the dish is an imposter. But for all the dogma and dissent, bouillabaisse was created by Provençal fishermen and was based not on conviction but on the catch of the day. Our version uses fillets rather than whole fish, and with all due respect to the mayor of Cassis, we also use a little white wine.

A true bouillabaisse takes time to make. While the recipe is hefty, it isn't complicated, and the broth can be prepared in advance and refrigerated overnight. Prior to serving bring it to a strong simmer and proceed to add the marinated fish.

***

SERVES 6 GENEROUSLY

INGREDIENTS

FOR THE MARINADE

- 2 tablespoons Pernod
- ½ teaspoon saffron threads
- 3 large tomatoes, cored and seeded
- ¼ cup olive oil
- 1½ pounds red snapper fillets
- 1½ pounds black bass fillets
- 1½ pounds cod fillets

FOR THE BROTH

- ½ cup olive oil
- 1 medium onion, sliced ⅛ inch thick
- 2 leeks, white parts only, well cleaned *(see page 144)* and sliced ⅛ inch thick
- 1 fennel bulb, sliced ⅛ inch thick
- 4 large garlic cloves, peeled and thinly sliced
- 1 tablespoon plus 1 pinch loosely packed saffron threads

- ¼ teaspoon red pepper flakes
- 1 bouquet garni *(see page 31)*
- 2 teaspoons salt
- 2 pounds fish bones, cut into 4-inch pieces and rinsed well
- 6 plum tomatoes, sliced
- 2 tablespoons tomato paste
- 1 cup dry white wine
- 4 Idaho potatoes, peeled and quartered
- 1 dozen mussels, cleaned and debearded
- 1 dozen littleneck clams (or substitute your favorite shellfish—shrimp, lobster, scallops)
- 1 tablespoon Pernod
- 1 baguette, sliced on the bias and toasted
- 1 cup Aïoli *(page 251)*

The day before serving, prepare the marinade for the fish: Bring the Pernod and ½ teaspoon of saffron to a boil in a small saucepan. Remove from the heat and let cool. In the bowl of a food processor, purée the 3 tomatoes and the ¼ cup olive oil, then pulse in the Pernod and saffron.

Cut the fish fillets into large pieces. Arrange the fish pieces in a large nonreactive casserole dish and pour over the marinade. Cover with plastic wrap and refrigerate overnight.

To make the broth: In an 8-quart stockpot, heat the ½ cup olive oil over a

medium flame. Add the onion, leeks, fennel, garlic, 1 tablespoon of the saffron, pepper flakes, bouquet garni, and salt. Cook until the vegetables are translucent but not brown, about 15 minutes. Raise the flame to high and add the fish bones. Stir frequently to free the bones of whatever meat clings to them. Cook for 10 minutes. Stir in the 6 sliced plum tomatoes, the tomato paste, white wine, and 2 quarts of water. Bring to a boil, then reduce to a strong simmer and cook for 20 minutes. Remove from the heat.

The flavor and body of the broth are greatly enriched by zipping an immersion blender along the bottom of the pot, but be careful not to trap any bones in the blade's protective cage. Move the blender smoothly along the bottom, whirling the broth and freeing any bits of fish that still cling to the bones.

Slowly pour the broth into a colander or large-holed strainer, catching the liquid in a large bowl. Use the back of a wooden spoon to firmly press the solids against the colander, forcing all broth and small bits of fish through the holes. Return the strained broth to the stockpot and discard the solids. (Cool and refrigerate if making in advance.)

Place the potatoes in a medium saucepan, cover with salted water, and add the

pinch of saffron. Bring to a boil and cook until tender, about 20 minutes. Drain.

Bring the strained broth to a boil and add the marinated fish along with the marinade, mussels, raw clams, drained potatoes, and a splash of Pernod. Cover with a tight-fitting lid and cook over medium heat only until the clams and mussels open, about 3 to 5 minutes.

Serve in deep bowls, each containing a selection of fish, shellfish, potatoes, and a toasted baguette slice. Serve the Aïoli in a small dish to be passed and spread on the baguettes.

MOULES À LA MARINIÈRE

A large crock of mussels seems glamorous late at night and workmanlike at lunch. Shiny and black, mussels evoke images of the Mediterranean, but they're also inexpensive, quick to cook, and go extremely well with beer. The broth itself is half the point, and the addition of crème fraîche lends a plump tanginess. Crusty bread or French Fries *(page 170)* are as important as a spoon.

SERVES 6 AS AN APPETIZER

In a large stockpot or Dutch oven, melt the butter over a low flame. Add the shallots, garlic, celery, and thyme. Gently sauté for about 15 minutes, until the vegetables are soft but not browned. Add the wine, pepper, and crème fraîche, and raise the flame to high. Once the liquid comes to a boil, add the mussels, stir gently, and cover with a tight-fitting lid. Cook for 3 minutes, or until the mussels open.

Add the parsley and stir gently. Serve in large bowls (remembering to discard any unopened mussels), with either crusty bread or French fries.

MUSSELS

Pick through mussels and discard any that are broken, or those that are wide open and have no spring in their hinge when pressed between thumb and forefinger. To clean, submerge in cool, clean water. Using your hands, rub each under running water, being sure to remove the "beard" or plantlike growth near the hinge (if in fact there is one: cultivation has almost entirely removed the need for this). Any type of mussel can be steamed in this, the classic, preparation. The green-lipped New Zealand, the Penn Cove (a Mediterranean mussel that's farmed near Seattle), or the Marbrand from Maine are now widely available. The small and succulent Prince Edward Island, which we use here, can be found at most fish counters.

INGREDIENTS

8 tablespoons unsalted butter

5 shallots, peeled and thinly sliced

4 garlic cloves, peeled and thinly sliced

2 celery stalks, thinly sliced on the bias

4 sprigs of thyme

1 cup dry white wine

2 teaspoons freshly ground white pepper

4 tablespoons crème fraîche

2 pounds Prince Edward Island mussels, well rinsed

20 sprigs of flat-leaf parsley, roughly chopped

WARM SALAD OF GRILLED TROUT

WITH SPINACH AND LENTILS

Served at lunch, dinner, or late-night, this well-rounded salad has been a favorite since the day we opened.

SERVES 4

In a small bowl, whisk together the honey and mustard to form a glaze. Set aside.

Prepare an ice-water bath in a large bowl and bring a medium pot of salted water to a boil. Blanch the asparagus until tender, 6 minutes. Drain and refresh them in the ice water to preserve their color. Drain again and set aside.

Heat the lentils over a low flame and keep warm.

Spray a grill or grill pan with nonstick spray and preheat until it's very hot (if using a grill pan, heat for at least 4 minutes). Dry the fillets and season the flesh sides with $\frac{1}{2}$ teaspoon of the salt and $\frac{1}{4}$ teaspoon of the pepper, then brush both sides with the olive oil. Place the fish, skin side down, on the grill and cook for 4 minutes. Flip the fish and brush the skin side with the reserved honey-mustard glaze. Continue to cook for 2 minutes. Hold the cooked trout aside.

Melt 3 tablespoons of the butter in a large sauté pan over medium heat. Add the walnuts and toast for about 3 minutes,

shaking the pan often to prevent burning. Season the nuts with $\frac{1}{4}$ teaspoon of salt, $\frac{1}{4}$ teaspoon of black pepper, and 3 tablespoons of the balsamic vinegar. Cook for 3 to 5 minutes, until the vinegar has reduced to a thick syrup that coats the nuts. Add the remaining tablespoon of butter and stir for an additional minute. Turn the flame down to low and add the asparagus.

In a small saucepan, bring the remaining $\frac{1}{2}$ cup of balsamic vinegar to a boil. Cook for about 3 minutes, until it has reduced down to 2 tablespoons.

Turn the flame off under the asparagus-walnut mixture and add the baby spinach along with a drizzle of the balsamic glaze. Gently toss to combine, and allow the heat of the pan to wilt the spinach.

Plate the salad by creating a small bed of the spinach-asparagus mixture in the center of the plate, surrounded by 3 dollops of warm lentils. Place 2 trout fillets, skin side up, on top of the spinach mixture. Drizzle with the balsamic glaze.

INGREDIENTS

¼ cup honey

¼ cup Dijon mustard

½ pound asparagus, stems trimmed, ends peeled, and cut into 2-inch pieces

1 cup cooked Lentils *(page 193)*

8 trout fillets, skin on

¾ teaspoon salt

½ teaspoon freshly ground pepper

⅓ cup olive oil

4 tablespoons unsalted butter

1 cup walnuts

3 tablespoons plus ½ cup balsamic vinegar

1 pound baby spinach, well rinsed and spun dry

SAUTÉED SKATE

WITH BROWN BUTTER, HARICOTS VERTS, AND HAZELNUTS

The bottom-feeding skate is a humble fish with a clean taste and sturdy flesh. This recipe calls for a classic brown-butter sauce, as well as a sprinkling of hazelnuts, which enhances the already nutty flavor of the dish. As always when buying fish, seek out firm flesh with no ammonia-like odor.

SERVES 6

⅓ cup hazelnuts	⅓ cup Wondra flour *(see page 59)*
1 pound haricots verts, stemmed	6 skate fillets
6 tablespoons olive oil	¼ teaspoon freshly ground black pepper
12 shallots, peeled and thinly sliced	12 tablespoons (1½ sticks) unsalted butter
1¼ teaspoons salt	2 tablespoons sherry vinegar

Preheat the oven to 325°F.

Spread the hazelnuts on a cookie sheet and toast in the oven for 4 to 5 minutes, or just until the nuts give off a pleasant aroma. Remove from the oven, roughly chop, and set aside.

Prepare an ice-water bath in a large bowl and bring a pot of salted water to a boil. Add the haricots verts and cook for 5 to 6 minutes, until tender. Strain, then submerge the beans in the ice bath to stop the cooking process. Strain again and set aside in the pot used to cook them.

Meanwhile, heat 3 tablespoons of the olive oil in a sauté pan over a low flame. Add the shallots and cook, without browning, for 8 to 10 minutes, until soft. Remove from the heat and add to the reserved haricots verts. Season with ½ teaspoon of the salt and toss.

The fish will be cooked in three batches, using a nonstick sauté pan. Place the flour in a shallow bowl. Season the whiter side of the skate fillets with ½ teaspoon salt and ¼ teaspoon pepper, then dredge that side in the flour, tapping off the excess. Over a high flame, heat 1 tablespoon of the olive oil in the sauté pan until it smokes. Add 2 skate wings to the pan, floured side down, and shake the pan so that the hot oil spreads and surrounds the fish (the oil will pool in the pan). Cook for 1½ minutes, turn, and cook the second side for 30 seconds. Remove from the heat and set the cooked fish aside on a cookie sheet. Repeat with the remaining fish, adding 1 tablespoon of olive oil to the pan each time before adding the next 2 fillets. Begin to reheat the haricots verts and shallots over a low flame.

When all the fish is cooked, keep the flame high and add the butter to the pan. The butter will melt, foam, then begin to brown. When it does, add the vinegar, reserved toasted hazelnuts, and ¼ teaspoon salt. Cool for 1 minute and remove from the heat.

Serve the skate over the haricots verts and spoon 2 tablespoons of brown butter over each fillet.

SOLE À LA MEUNIÈRE

The perfect sole meunière is golden brown, which is a result of a harmonious balance between the brown butter and the lemon. It's a fast and simple dish and characteristic of classic bistro cooking.

SERVES 6

Preheat the oven to 300°F.

Dry the sole fillets and season both sides with ¾ teaspoon of the salt and the white pepper. Dredge the fillets in the flour and shake off the excess.

Heat 2 tablespoons of the oil in a large nonstick sauté pan over a medium-high flame. When the oil smokes, add 2 fillets and cook for 3 minutes on each side. Transfer to a baking sheet, place in the warm oven, and continue with the next 2 fillets. Add oil as necessary, heating to

the smoking point before adding the fillets. Repeat with the remaining 2 fillets.

Transfer all the cooked fillets to the oven and wipe the sauté pan clean with a paper towel. Add the butter to the pan over a medium flame. It will melt, foam, subside, and then begin to bubble again and turn a nutty brown. Add the lemon juice, parsley, the remaining ½ teaspoon of salt, and several grindings of white pepper to taste. Serve the fillets on warm plates with the sauce spooned over.

INGREDIENTS

6 Dover sole fillets
1¼ teaspoons salt
½ teaspoon freshly ground white pepper, plus more to taste
¾ cup flour (*Wondra or all-purpose; see page 59*)

6 tablespoons vegetable oil
12 tablespoons (1½ sticks) unsalted butter
Juice of 2 lemons (¼ cup)
¼ cup flat-leaf parsley

DOVER SOLE

Dover sole is an expensive fish imported from Europe. Firm and flat, it is perfect for pan-frying.

FLOUNDER À LA PROVENÇALE

As the name implies, tomatoes, garlic, and olive oil are staples of this bright and pleasant dish. Although the recipe calls for flounder, in fact any white flaky fish would do well with the same treatment.

SERVES 6

PHOTOGRAPH BY CHRISTOPHER HIRSHEIMER

INGREDIENTS

6 whole flounders (nearly
   6 pounds), cleaned and
   skinned
1 teaspoon salt
   Freshly ground white pepper
   Wondra flour, for dredging
9 tablespoons plus ½ cup
   olive oil

3 small garlic cloves, finely
   diced
6 tomatoes, peeled, seeded,
   and cut into ½-inch dice
   (see page 244)
¼ cup chopped flat-leaf
   parsley

Dry and season the fish with ½ teaspoon of salt and several grindings of white pepper. Dredge in the flour and lightly shake off the excess. Add 3 tablespoons of the olive oil to a large sauté pan (cast iron is ideal) and set over a medium-high flame. When the oil starts to smoke, add 2 of the fish and brown for 4 minutes per side, aiming for a crisp brown crust. Transfer the cooked fish to a warm platter and hold until all the fish are cooked (or hold in a 200°F. oven). Cook the remaining fish in the same manner, wiping the sauté pan clean and replenishing the oil each time.

Reduce the heat to low and add the remaining ½ cup of olive oil to the pan. Add the garlic and cook until soft and translucent but not brown, about 2 minutes, stirring frequently. Add the diced tomatoes and parsley and stir well to combine. Cook for about 1 minute, just to lightly warm the tomatoes. Season with ¼ teaspoon of salt and a few grindings of white pepper. Plate the flounder and spoon the sauce generously over the fish.

WONDRA FLOUR

We find Wondra flour by Gold Medal yields the best results when pan-frying fish. It has a fine blend of wheat and barley that creates a very smooth and crispy crust.

SOLE EN PAPILLOTE

This is a restaurant dish that easily adapts to the home kitchen: The delicate fish and aromatic vegetables are portioned, cooked, and served together in parchment packets. The paper creates a steamy environment in which the fish stays moist and the flavors intermingle. This is a naturally low-fat way to cook since little oil is needed. As chefs we prefer to serve it with a sauce of shallots, wine, vermouth, and butter. If guided by your conscience, feel free to skip the sauce and serve with Rice Pilaf *(page 192)* and a salad.

SERVES 6

Preheat the oven to 400°F.

Heat the olive oil in a medium skillet. Add the matchstick carrots, leek, and celery and cook over moderate heat until just softened, about 5 minutes. Remove to a bowl with a slotted spoon, and season with ¼ teaspoon of the salt and a few grindings of pepper. Add the mushrooms to the pan and sauté for 7 minutes, until brown. Remove the mushrooms to the same bowl and set aside.

In a medium saucepan, combine the shallots, thyme, wine, and vermouth. Cook over medium heat until the liquid has reduced to about 3 tablespoons and has a syrupy consistency, about 5 to 7 minutes.

Remove the thyme sprigs. Keep warm over low heat.

Cut 6 sheets of parchment paper into 12-inch circles. Season the sole fillets with ½ teaspoon salt and ¼ teaspoon white pepper. Take a sheet of parchment and fold it in half to create a crease. Place a few carrot, leek, and celery matchsticks on one side of the fold. Place a fillet on the julienned vegetables, and then add a few of the quartered mushrooms. To seal up the packet, fold the other half of the parchment over the top so the edges meet. Start at the left side of the half circle, folding the edges up at ½-inch intervals and crimping the end closed. The finished

INGREDIENTS

½ cup olive oil

2 carrots, cut into 3-inch matchsticks

2 leeks, white part only, well cleaned *(see page 144)* and cut into 3-inch matchsticks

2 celery stalks, cut into 3-inch matchsticks

1¼ teaspoons salt

¼ teaspoon freshly ground white pepper, plus more to taste

¼ pound small white mushrooms, stems discarded, caps quartered

2 shallots, minced

14 whole sprigs of thyme, plus 1 tablespoon chopped

½ cup dry white wine

¼ cup vermouth

6 sole fillets, 6 to 8 ounces each

1 pound unsalted butter, cubed

packet will look like a large paper empanada. Transfer the packet to a baking sheet and continue with the remaining fish and parchment. When all the packets are on the baking sheet, brush them with olive oil and slide into the preheated oven for 10 to 17 minutes. The packets will begin to brown and puff with air.

Meanwhile, complete the sauce: Begin whisking the cubes of butter, one cube at a time, into the warm reduction of white wine and vermouth over very low heat. Don't let the mixture approach a boil or it will separate. Let each cube incorporate before adding the next. This can take up to 15 minutes. When finished, the sauce should be thick and creamy. Stir in the chopped thyme, ½ teaspoon of salt, and several grindings of white pepper. Keep warm over a simmering water bath.

Remove the packets from the oven and transfer each to a plate. Using a pair of scissors, cut the crimped edge off and discard. Serve with the warm sauce spooned over.

EN PAPILLOTE

This is a method of cooking that's almost more about the arranging: The most significant technique is the creasing and folding of the paper envelopes so that they stay tightly closed during cooking. Cheating is available in the form of a staple—just one with the last fold—but be very sure to carefully remove after cooking. Aluminum foil can replace parchment in the method, but not in effect; the scorched parchment envelopes puff dramatically in the oven.

WHOLE ROASTED DORADE

WITH FENNEL, OLIVES, AND LEMON

Roasting a whole fish over fennel epitomizes everything that's wonderful about Mediterranean cooking. And so it should, for this is the land where fennel grows wild. Dorade comes fresh from the ocean, and simplicity rules supreme.

***

SERVES 4

Preheat the oven to 400°F.

Prepare an ice-water bath in a large bowl and bring a pot of salted water to a boil. Trim the stem end of each fennel bulb and remove the outer layer. Cut each bulb in half and then into ½-inch slices. Blanch for 10 minutes, drain, then transfer to the ice bath. Drain and set aside.

Line a baking sheet with foil. Toss the fennel, a few of the lemon slices, garlic, 12 sprigs of thyme, 4 sprigs of oregano, and bay leaves with olive oil. Spread the fennel and herbs on the foil-lined baking sheet.

Rub a tablespoon of olive oil over each dorade and then season them on both sides, and in the cavity, with the salt and pepper. Stuff the cavity of each fish with 2 sprigs of thyme, 2 lemon slices, and 1 sprig of oregano. Lay the fish over the bed of fennel and garlic, then top with the sliced lemons and olives. Drizzle the lemon juice and remaining olive oil over the fish and transfer the tray to the middle rack of the preheated oven. Cook for about 20 minutes. Test for doneness by cutting into the flesh at the spine; it should be white and pull away from the bone.

Run a long pointed knife, starting behind the head, along the spine and under the top fillet. Lift the fillet onto a plate. Then run a spatula under the exposed bony skeleton. Lift and discard, and then plate the bottom fillet. Serve with the fennel, olives, lemons, and chopped parsley.

INGREDIENTS

- 4 fennel bulbs
- 6 lemons, 4 sliced and 2 juiced
- 2 heads of garlic, cloves separated, skins on
- 20 sprigs of thyme
- 8 sprigs of oregano
- 4 bay leaves, each broken in half
- ½ cup olive oil

- 4 dorade, about 1¼ pounds each, scaled and gutted, rinsed and dried
- 1 teaspoon salt
- ½ teaspoon freshly ground black pepper
- ¼ pound mixed olives (your favorites)
- 2 tablespoons chopped flat-leaf parsley

GRILLED MACKEREL

WITH CABBAGE

Mackerel, in French *maquereau* or *lisette,* is a lowly fish that rises to great heights when grilled thanks to its oily texture and distinctive flavor. Set against waxy potatoes and cabbage, this is a wonderful combination of earthy ingredients.

SERVES 6

Bring a large pot of salted water to a boil. Slice the cabbage as you would for coleslaw: julienne the leaves into thin strips. Cook the sliced cabbage in the boiling salted water for 3 to 5 minutes, until tender. Drain and set aside.

In a medium bowl, combine the crème fraîche, capers, cornichons, shallots, and tarragon; stir well to combine. Mix ¼ cup of the dressing with the cabbage—just enough to coat the leaves. Chill until ready to use, along with the remaining dressing.

Boil the potatoes in their skins in a fresh pot of salted boiling water until they're tender but still hold their shape, about 20 minutes. Drain and set aside.

Season the mackerel with the salt and pepper. Brush the fillets with olive oil and set skin side down on a grill over moderate heat. Cook for 3 to 5 minutes, until the flesh side turns opaque. Alternatively, heat a casserole dish under a broiler for about 3 minutes. Brush the fillets generously with olive oil and place in the hot casserole dish, skin side down, for 3 minutes.

Slice the warm potatoes into ½-inch slices. Arrange on plates and top with the dressed cabbage. Add the mackerel, skin side up, with a bit of dressing spooned over and around.

INGREDIENTS

¼ head napa cabbage

½ cup crème fraîche

3 tablespoons capers

3 tablespoons chopped cornichons

2 shallots, finely chopped

2 tablespoons chopped tarragon leaves

3 medium Yukon gold potatoes (about 1 pound), peeled

6 mackerel fillets (about 1½ pounds), cleaned and bones removed

1 teaspoon salt

½ teaspoon pepper

2 tablespoons olive oil

COD MITONNÉE

Soups thickened by yesterday's baguette are classic peasant cuisine. Here, toasted bread is the foil for a delicate slab of cod and an aromatic broth. Served in a bowl, this is a substantial but light meal. We melt a bit of Gruyère on the crouton for a sharp richness, but that could be left out; just be sure to adjust the seasoning of the broth, adding a bit more salt.

SERVES 6

Preheat the oven to 350°F.

Heat ¼ cup of the olive oil over a medium-high flame in a Dutch oven. Add the onions, garlic, and thyme and sauté for 30 minutes, until the ingredients have turned golden brown. Add the white wine and the Chicken Stock. Turn the flame down to medium-low and simmer for 30 minutes.

Toast the bread in the oven on a baking sheet, and then top with some grated Gruyère. Run under the broiler to melt the cheese. Keep the oven temperature at 350°F.

When the broth has cooked for 30 minutes, turn the flame down very low. Heat the remaining ¼ cup of olive oil in a large nonstick sauté pan. Season the cod fillets

with ½ teaspoon salt and ¼ teaspoon white pepper. When the oil is smoking, add 3 of the cod fillets and sear on each side for 3 minutes. Transfer them to a baking sheet and then sear the remaining 3 fillets. Transfer the baking sheet to the oven and cook for 5 to 7 minutes, until the cod is opaque and just beginning to flake.

Meanwhile, add the Swiss chard to the Chicken Stock along with the White Beans, if using, fines herbes, and diced tomatoes. Season the broth with salt and pepper to taste.

Ladle the broth and bean mixture into 6 shallow bowls. Set a toast in each bowl and then top with a cod fillet.

INGREDIENTS

½ cup olive oil

2¼ large yellow onions, peeled and sliced ¼ inch thick

3 garlic cloves, peeled and thinly sliced

5 sprigs of thyme

¾ cup white wine

5 cups Chicken Stock *(page 230)*

6 slices of country bread

6 ounces Gruyère, grated

6 cod fillets

½ teaspoon salt, plus more to taste

¼ teaspoon freshly ground white pepper, plus more to taste

2 cups loosely packed Swiss chard leaves, torn into bite-size pieces

White Beans *(page 196)*, optional

1 tablespoon fines herbes *(see page 87)*

3 tomatoes, peeled, seeded, and diced *(see page 244)*

COD WITH COCKLES

AND PARSLEY

Against the clean flavor of cod, briny cockles are a reminder of the ocean. This well-composed main course looks like more effort than it actually is.

SERVES 6

COCKLES

Cockles are tiny green-shelled bivalves that can be eaten raw but are more frequently served steamed. Order them ahead of time from the fishmonger. If cockles aren't available, try Manilla clams or little-necks. Rinse well before using and, as with clams, discard any with shells that don't close when touched.

INGREDIENTS

2 cups of flat-leaf parsley leaves

3 Yukon gold potatoes, peeled and cut into ½-inch dice

6 tablespoons unsalted butter

3 leeks, white parts only, quartered, sliced ½ inch thick, and rinsed well *(see page 144)*

Salt

Freshly ground black pepper

2 cups white wine

½ teaspoon chopped fresh thyme

1 clove garlic, minced (about 1 teaspoon)

¼ cup olive oil

6 cod fillets (about 8 ounces each), skin on if possible

1 pound cockles (about 36 of them)

Preheat the oven to 375°F.

Bring a medium saucepan of salted water to a boil. Add the parsley and blanch over high heat for 2 minutes. Remove with a slotted spoon, reserving ½ cup of the cooking water. Place in a blender along with the reserved cooking liquid and purée. Refrigerate until needed.

Bring more salted water to a boil in a large pot. Drop the diced potatoes in and cook until tender, 8 to 10 minutes; try not to overcook as the potatoes will lose their shape. Drain through a colander and set aside.

Melt 2 tablespoons of the butter in a large sauté pan (one with a tight-fitting lid) over medium heat. When the foam subsides, add the leeks and cook until soft and translucent but not brown, about 5 minutes. Transfer to a bowl and season with ¼ teaspoon of salt and freshly ground pepper. Set aside.

Pour the wine into the sauté pan, along with the thyme and garlic. The cockles will be steamed in this while the fish cooks in the oven, so hold on the stovetop over low heat until needed.

Heat 3 tablespoons of the olive oil in a large (preferably nonstick) sauté pan over a high flame. Dry the cod fillets and season with the salt and pepper. When the oil smokes, add 3 of the cod fillets; shake the pan to distribute the oil. Let the fillets brown, undisturbed, for 3 to 4 minutes. Transfer to a plate while the other 3 fillets are seared in the same way, replenishing the oil if necessary. Flip the fish and return the first 3 fillets to the pan, seared side up. Sear the other side for 2 minutes, then transfer all the fish to the preheated oven. Cook for 8 minutes, until the flesh is opaque and just starting to flake.

Gently heat the potatoes and leeks in a sauté pan. Raise the heat to high under the white wine, and add the cockles. When the cockles open their shells, about 3 to 4 minutes, add the reserved potatoes and leeks and the remaining 4 tablespoons of butter. Replace the lid and cook for 1 to 2 minutes. Season with ¼ teaspoon of salt and 2 to 3 grindings of pepper. A minute before serving, add the parsley purée. Spoon into shallow bowls, top with a cod fillet, and eat with a spoon.

COD WITH LOBSTER,

CHICKPEAS, AND SAUCE AMÉRICAINE

The classic Sauce Américaine was created in Paris in the late nineteenth century by a chef who'd just returned from a stint in Chicago. The international name impressed his Parisian diners and probably did wonders for the image of American food at the time. Topping off a dish of cod and lobster, Sauce Américaine continues to impress. This is a somewhat involved preparation, making it extremely suitable to cooking in concert. Be sure to soak the chickpeas the night before.

SERVES 6

Soak the chickpeas in a large bowl of water overnight. The next day, strain and transfer to a saucepan. Fill with water (twice the volume of the chickpeas), and set over a high flame. When the water comes to a boil, lower to a simmer and cook for 45 minutes, or until the chickpeas are tender. Strain and set aside.

Prepare the Sauce Américaine, reserving the cooked lobster meat.

Dry the cod fillets with paper towels. Season the flesh side with the salt and pepper. Heat 3 tablespoons of the vegetable oil in a large nonstick pan over a high flame until it begins to smoke. Reduce the flame to medium and add

3 fillets to the pan, skin side down. After placing the fish in the pan, give the pan a quick shake to make sure the fish doesn't stick. Cook for 5 minutes, flip to the flesh side, and cook for 2 minutes. Hold in a warm oven while the remaining fillets are cooked. Replenish the oil if necessary.

Add the cooked chickpeas to the Sauce Américaine and heat in a medium saucepan. Add the reserved lobster chunks and the tarragon and heat for about a minute more.

To serve, spoon the heated sauce (about 3 tablespoons or so) into the center of 6 shallow serving bowls, and place a piece of sautéed cod on top of each.

INGREDIENTS

1 cup dried chickpeas, picked over, stones removed

Sauce Américaine *(page 246)*, including lobster meat

6 cod fillets (about 6 ounces each), with skin on

½ teaspoon salt

¼ teaspoon freshly ground white pepper

6 tablespoons vegetable oil or clarified butter

4 sprigs of tarragon, leaves removed from stems and chopped

GRILLED SWORDFISH

WITH BEURRE NOIR

The nutty dark butter that accompanies this grilled swordfish is enriched with raisins, capers, and pequillo peppers—just a few moderate changes to the classic beurre noir preparation. Serve with Sautéed Broccoli Rabe with Olive Oil and Garlic *(page 200)*.

SERVES 6

Rub the olive oil over the swordfish and season with the salt and several turns of a peppermill.

Heat a grill or grill pan to medium-high. When hot, add the swordfish steaks and cook for about 4 minutes per side for a moist and medium doneness; test by peeking into the center of the steak with the tip of a sharp knife—the fish should be tender, juicy, and opaque. As always with fish, undercooking is preferable to overcooking. Plate the fish while the beurre noir is completed.

Melt the butter in a sauté pan over a medium flame. It will foam, then begin to turn a dark brown, nutty color. Add the capers, raisins, peppers, pine nuts, and parsley. Swirl the butter and then add the lemon juice.

Spoon the buerre noir over the swordfish and serve immediately.

INGREDIENTS

¼ cup olive oil

6 swordfish steaks (about 1 inch thick)

½ teaspoon salt
   Freshly ground black pepper

¼ pound (1 stick) unsalted butter

2 tablespoons capers

3 tablespoons golden raisins

2 tablespoons preserved pequillo peppers

2 tablespoons pine nuts

2 tablespoons chopped flat-leaf parsley
   Juice of ½ lemon (about 2 tablespoons)

HALIBUT À LA BARIGOULE

A broth of braised artichokes and basil purée surrounds this tender halibut and makes for a hearty dish.

SERVES 6

INGREDIENTS

2 cups loosely packed basil leaves	12 baby artichokes, cleaned and thinly sliced
½ teaspoon coriander seeds	1 cup white wine
½ teaspoon black peppercorns	5 cups Chicken Stock (page 230)
1 bay leaf	1 cup White Beans (page 196), optional
½ cup plus 3 tablespoons olive oil	6 halibut fillets
½ pint pearl onions, peeled	¼ teaspoon freshly ground white pepper
2 cloves garlic, minced	
1½ teaspoons salt	
3 medium carrots, cut into ¼-inch half-moons	

Prepare an ice-water bath in a medium bowl and bring a medium saucepan of salted water to a boil. Add the basil and blanch for 1 minute. Strain, plunge the leaves into the ice bath, and reserve ¼ cup of the cooking water. Remove the leaves from the ice water and squeeze to remove as much liquid as possible. Place in the work bowl of a food processor along with the reserved ¼ cup of liquid and process until smooth, green, and bright. Refrigerate until needed.

Wrap the coriander seeds, peppercorns, and bay leaf in cheesecloth to make a sachet. Set aside. Heat ¼ cup of olive oil in a large sauté pan over a medium flame. Add the onions and garlic along with 1 teaspoon of salt and sauté until the onions are soft and translucent, about 5 minutes. Add the carrots and herb sachet and cook for 5 minutes.

When the carrots have softened, add the sliced artichokes and the wine. Bring to a simmer and reduce the liquid by half, about 5 minutes. Add the Chicken Stock and simmer for 30 minutes. Stir in the cooked White Beans, if using, and keep warm over a low flame while the halibut is cooked.

Preheat the oven to 400°F.

Dry the halibut fillets and season with the remaining ½ teaspoon of salt and the ¼ teaspoon white pepper.

Use 2 large sauté pans to cook the fish or, if using 1 pan, cook the fish in 2 batches. Heat 3 tablespoons of olive oil in the sauté pan until the oil smokes. Place 3 of the fillets in the pan and cook for 2 minutes per side. Transfer the pan to the preheated oven to finish cooking for 5 minutes, or until the fish just begins to flake around the edges.

Just before serving, remove the spice sachet from the broth, add the basil purée, and add the remaining ¼ cup of olive oil. Stir well to combine, and spoon the warm barigoule sauce into 6 shallow bowls, with a halibut fillet in the center.

ROASTED HALIBUT

WITH CRUSHED POTATOES, ALMONDS, AND TOMATOES

Definitely *not* a brasserie classic, this is a souvenir from our days working with Chef Daniel Boulud. With the crunch of almonds and the sharpness of Sweet-and-Sour Shallots, this dish feels both light and substantial. We use halibut for its firm flesh and sweet, mellow flavor, but cod is an acceptable stand-in.

SERVES 6

Preheat the oven to 400°F.

Spread the blanched almonds in a single layer on a cookie sheet and toast in the oven for 3 minutes, or just until fragrant. Set aside.

Pat the halibut fillets dry with paper towels. Season both sides of the fish with the salt and pepper. Heat a 12-inch nonstick sauté pan over a high flame. Add the vegetable oil and heat until it begins to smoke. Add 3 of the fillets and sear for 2 minutes on each side. Remove and set aside while you repeat with the remaining 3 fillets. When those have been seared, return the first group to the pan and trans-

fer all the fish to the oven for 3 minutes to finish. The cooking process will continue outside of the oven while the rest of the dish is assembled.

Heat the Crushed Potatoes in a microwave or in a double boiler. In a small saucepan, combine the olive oil, Sweet-and-Sour Shallots, and tomatoes. Set over a low flame and heat until warm, then swirl in the parsley.

To serve, lay the halibut fillets over a bed of Crushed Potatoes, and spoon the warm shallot–tomato sauce over and around. Garnish with the almonds.

INGREDIENTS

¾ cup blanched almonds

6 halibut fillets, about
  6 ounces each

1 teaspoon salt

½ teaspoon freshly ground
  white pepper

3 tablespoons vegetable oil
Crushed Potatoes *(page 175)*

¾ cup extra-virgin olive oil

6 tablespoons Sweet-and-Sour
  Shallots *(page 242)*

3 large tomatoes, peeled,
  seeded, and diced *(see
  page 244)*

18 sprigs of flat-leaf parsley,
  roughly chopped

MUSTARD-CRUSTED SALMON

WITH LENTILS AND SWEET GARLIC JUS

With its earthy and satisfying ingredients, this classic dish embodies the spirit of bistro cooking. The presentation may lack refinement, but it has undeniable style. Lentils, a staple of the French kitchen, grow near the celebrated mustard fields of Dijon, and these two ingredients act as the perfect accompaniment to the salmon. The Sweet Garlic Jus adds further depth to the dish.

SERVES 6

Preheat the oven to 500°F.

Season the salmon fillets on both sides with the salt and pepper. On the rounded side of each fillet, spread 2 teaspoons of Dijon mustard, followed by a sprinkling of 1 teaspoon of bread crumbs. Use your fingers to press the crumbs into the mustard.

Heat a large, ovenproof, nonstick sauté pan over a high flame and add the vegetable oil. When the oil begins to smoke, add the salmon, mustard-coated side of the fish down. Lower the flame to medium. Sear the fish for 2 minutes, until the mustard and bread crumbs form a crust, then turn to sear the second side for 1 minute more. Transfer the pan to the oven to finish cooking for 3 minutes for medium-rare, or 4 minutes for medium. Plate the salmon alongside the warm lentils, and drizzle both with the Sweet Garlic Jus.

INGREDIENTS

6 salmon fillets, about 7 ounces each

1½ teaspoons salt

½ teaspoon freshly ground black pepper

¼ cup Dijon mustard

6 teaspoons dry bread crumbs

2 tablespoons vegetable oil
Lentils *(page 193)*

1 cup Sweet Garlic Jus *(page 233)*, optional

KOULIBIAC

Described as a four-corner fish pie by the Russian novelist Nikolai Gogol, Koulibiac is undeniably grand. The Balthazar dining room, also grand, feels like one of the few places in New York where you might find this showy, old-fashioned dish. Layers of salmon, divided by rice and wrapped in puff pastry, break down into a surprisingly simple process of sautéing a few different components, stacking them up, and wrapping them in store-bought pastry. To ensure that each slice is flavorful throughout, season each component separately. Serve as a main course, an appetizer, or a luncheon dish.

SERVES 6

Trim the salmon fillets so that they're the same size, about 6 by 8 inches. Season each piece with ¼ teaspoon salt per side and a few grindings of white pepper. In a large sauté pan, heat 2 tablespoons of the vegetable oil over a high flame until it smokes. Sear one fillet at a time, for 1½ minutes per side. Repeat with the other fillet, then set aside, or wrap and refrigerate.

INGREDIENTS

2 salmon fillets, each 8 inches long, each about 18 to 20 ounces

Salt

Freshly ground white pepper

7 tablespoons vegetable oil

½ pound white button mushrooms, thinly sliced

1 onion, halved and thinly sliced

¼ head of savoy cabbage, cored and thinly sliced

1 tightly packed cup spinach leaves, cut into ½-inch strips

2 tablespoons chopped dill

½ cup uncooked white rice

2 shallots, peeled and thinly sliced

1 garlic clove, peeled and sliced

1 cup dry white wine

1 cup heavy cream

½ cup whole milk

2 sheets of puff pastry (1 package of Pepperidge Farm, or 2 packages of Dufour)

All-purpose flour

1 large egg, beaten

Discard the oil in the sauté pan, wipe with a paper towel, and add 3 fresh table-spoons of the vegetable oil. Over a high flame, heat the oil, and add the mush-rooms. Sauté for 4 minutes, until browned, and then cool and drain in a colander. When cool enough to handle, season the mushrooms with a pinch of salt and a few turns of the pepper mill. Use paper towels to dry the mushrooms well and then chop the slices into a mince (or *duxelles*). Set aside.

Add 2 more tablespoons of the vegetable oil to the sauté pan and set over a medium flame. Add the sliced onion and cook until soft but not brown, about 5 minutes. Add the cabbage along with 1 cup of water. Stir, cover, and cook for 20 min-utes, stirring occasionally. Remove from the heat and add the spinach, stirring or tossing with tongs until the leaves wilt. Pour into a colander to drain, and then add 2 tablespoons of the chopped dill to the mixture, along with ¼ teaspoon of salt and some freshly ground pepper. Use your hands to combine well, and then squeeze

with paper towels to dry the mixture as much as possible. Set aside.

Meanwhile, place the rice in a medium saucepan with 1½ cups of water. Place over a medium flame, stir once, and cover with a tight-fitting lid. Cook until the water has all but disappeared, about 18 minutes. Remove from the heat, let rest 5 minutes, covered, and then fluff with a fork. Set aside.

Prepare the sauce that will be spooned over the sliced pastry: In a small saucepan, combine the shallots, garlic, and wine with the cream and milk. Bring to a foamy simmer and cook over medium heat until the cream has reduced to 1 cup, about 5 minutes. Strain and re-serve the cream.

To prepare the puff pastry, have 2 cookie sheets ready along with 2 sheets of parch-ment paper. Take 1 sheet of pastry out of the refrigerator at a time. Lightly flour a work surface and a rolling pin, and roll the dough (which is generally about ¼ inch thick out of the package) to a ⅛-inch

thickness. When finished, roll the dough around the rolling pin (like a window shade) to transfer it from the floured surface to a parchment-lined cookie sheet. Cover the dough with the second piece of parchment, and hold it in the refrigerator while rolling out the other piece of puff pastry. Again, transfer the rolled-out dough onto the second piece of parchment and hold both sheets of dough in the refrigerator for at least 10 minutes to rest before constructing the Koulibiac.

Preheat the oven to 350°F. In a large bowl, combine the onion-cabbage mixture and the cooked rice to form the stuffing.

Leave 1 sheet of puff pastry and parchment in the refrigerator. Place the other sheet with its parchment lining onto the cookie sheet, in front of you, with the rectangle of dough going from left to right. Spread half of the stuffing in the center, forming a rectangle the same size as the salmon fillets. Place one salmon fillet over the stuffing (spine side facing up), and evenly spread the mushrooms over the fillet. Lay the second salmon fillet over the mushrooms, spine side facing down, with the thicker half of the top fillet over the thinner half of the bottom, to level things out. Spread the remaining stuffing over the top, and pack as much as possible into the gap between the two pieces of fish.

Brush the beaten egg on the border around the rectangle of salmon and stuffing. Lay the other piece of puff pastry (without its parchment lining) over the stacked fillets and pull the dough as tight and smooth as possible (try to keep any folds that occur to the corners). Use your fingertips to press the top sheet of dough into the bottom sheet snugly all around. Use a sharp knife to trim away all but a ½-inch border of dough. Again, use your fingertips to form a snug crimping and sealing of the dough all the way around. Brush the egg wash over the entire Koulibiac, refrigerate for 10 minutes, and then apply another coat of egg wash for a deep golden finish.

Bake for 20 minutes, rotating it in the oven halfway through the cooking time. Meanwhile, begin to warm the cream sauce over a low flame. Remove the Koulibiac from the oven when the pastry is dark and shiny. Use the parchment paper to slide it onto a cutting board. With a sharp knife (or an electric knife if you have one) slice off the ends of the pastry, or what would be called the heels if it were a loaf of bread. Cut 1-inch slices and use a cake server to transfer the slices to plates, and spoon the warm cream sauce over and around the slices.

SALMON FILLETS

When purchasing the fish, ask the fishmonger to cut the fillets fresh from a whole side of salmon. Ask for the fillets closest to the head, which will be straight sided and evenly sized, unlike the sloping fillets near the tail.

SALMON WITH RADICCHIO,

MUSHROOMS, AND SOFT POLENTA

Read this recipe through before undertaking it because there are a few components to the dish. The best course of action would be to make the Roast Chicken Jus *(page 232)* and then the Vinegar Jus (recipe follows), which can be done the day before. The mushrooms and radicchio can then be cooked and the polenta prepared, finishing up with the sautéing of the salmon.

SERVES 6

Preheat the oven to 375°F.

In a large sauté pan, heat ¼ cup of the olive oil until it begins to smoke. Add the mushrooms and sauté for 5 to 7 minutes, until the mushrooms take on a nutty color. Add the minced shallot and sauté for another 2 minutes. Add the radicchio and sauté just long enough for the leaves to wilt, about 1 minute. Season with ½ teaspoon of the salt and the ¼ teaspoon of black pepper and toss with the fines herbes. Set aside while the salmon is sautéed.

Heat 3 tablespoons of the olive oil in a large, preferably nonstick or cast iron, ovenproof pan. Dry the salmon fillets and season them with ½ teaspoon of the salt and the ¼ teaspoon of white pepper.

When the oil starts to smoke, add 3 salmon fillets and cook for 3 minutes on each side, or until a crisp brown crust forms. Remove to a plate while the remaining fillets are seared in the same manner. Return all the fillets to the pan, browned sides up, and transfer to the preheated oven for 5 to 6 minutes for medium doneness.

Heat the Vinegar Jus over a medium flame and swirl the butter into the warm sauce. To serve, spoon the polenta onto warm plates or into shallow bowls. Top with a seared salmon fillet and then garnish with the radicchio and mushrooms. Drizzle the Vinegar Jus over and around.

INGREDIENTS

¼ cup plus 6 tablespoons
    olive oil
6 ounces white button
    mushrooms, stemmed,
    cleaned, and quartered
6 ounces shiitake mushrooms,
    stemmed, cleaned, and
    quartered
1 shallot, minced (about
    1 tablespoon)
2 heads of radicchio, cored
    and cut into 1-inch pieces
1 teaspoon salt

¼ teaspoon freshly ground
    black pepper
1 tablespoon fines herbes
    (see Note)
6 salmon fillets (about
    6 ounces each)
¼ teaspoon freshly ground
    white pepper
    Vinegar Jus *(recipe follows)*
3 tablespoons unsalted butter
2 cups soft Mascarpone-
    Parmesan Polenta
    (page 185)

VINEGAR JUS

MAKES 2 CUPS

3 tablespoons olive oil
2 shallots, thinly sliced
1 sprig of fresh thyme
¼ teaspoon whole black
    peppercorns
¼ cup sherry vinegar
¼ cup balsamic vinegar
1 cup Roast Chicken Jus
    (page 232)
    Salt and freshly ground
    black pepper to taste

Heat the olive oil in a small
saucepan over a medium flame. Add
the shallots, thyme, and peppercorns. Sauté for 5 minutes, or until
the shallots start to brown. Add both
vinegars, raise the flame to high, and
reduce the liquid by half, about 3
minutes. Reduce the flame to
medium, add the chicken jus, and
bring to a simmer. Skim if necessary.
Reduce the liquid once again, this
time by a third, about 5 minutes.
Taste to correct the seasoning,
adding salt and pepper as necessary.
Hold the sauce aside, or refrigerate
if making ahead of time.

FINES HERBES

*Like herbes de Provence, this is a name for an en-
semble of herbs: Fresh parsley, chervil, chives, and
tarragon are chopped together and treated as a
single ingredient.*

MONKFISH GRAND-MÈRE

The term *grand-mère*, or "grandmother," indicates a recipe that includes bacon, mushrooms, potatoes, and onions. It's a rustic preparation most often seen with poultry or meat, but it adapts wonderfully to the firm and lean texture of monkfish. Prepare all but the last step ahead of time, then cook the fish just minutes before serving.

SERVES 6

Bring a medium saucepan of salted water to a boil. Add the pearl onions and cook for 10 minutes. Drain and set aside.

Meanwhile, put the potatoes in another medium saucepan of salted water. Bring to a boil and cook until tender, about 15 minutes. Drain, and when they're cool enough to handle, remove the skins. Slice into ¼-inch disks.

Place the bacon in a large dry sauté pan over medium heat and cook until brown, 5 to 7 minutes. Remove with a slotted spoon and set aside. Pour the fat out of the pan, wipe clean with a paper towel, and add 2 tablespoons of the olive oil. Heat over a medium-high flame, and as the oil begins to smoke, add the mushrooms, working in batches to avoid crowding the pan. Stir gently and cook until the mushrooms are soft and brown, about 5 minutes. Add ¼ teaspoon salt and set aside. Replenish the pan with 2 table-spoons olive oil and heat until it smokes. Add the potato slices and sauté until they're brown and crisp, about 5 minutes. Season with ¼ teaspoon salt.

Dry the monkfish pieces with paper towels and season with ¼ teaspoon salt and several grindings of pepper. Heat 2 table-spoons of olive oil in a large, nonstick sauté pan over a medium-high flame. When the oil begins to smoke, add half the monkfish. (If using a nonstick pan, the oil will pool; when placing the fish in the pan, give each piece a slide through the oil.) Cook until golden brown, about 2 minutes per side. Repeat the process with the rest of the fish. When all the pieces have been cooked, add them back to the pan. Add the reserved mushrooms, potatoes, and bacon, along with the parsley and chicken jus. Bring to a simmer, correct the seasonings, and serve in a large, deep platter or casserole.

INGREDIENTS

6 ounces pearl onions, peeled

10 ounces fingerling potatoes

8 ounces slab bacon, cut into ½-inch dice

8 tablespoons olive oil

1 pound wild mushrooms (porcini, shiitake, hen-of-the-woods), stemmed and sliced ¼ inch thick

¾ teaspoon salt

2 pounds monkfish fillets
Freshly ground black pepper

6 sprigs of flat-leaf parsley, chopped

2 cups Roast Chicken Jus (page 232)

STRIPED BASS

WITH TOMATO AND SAFFRON

For those of us with busy lives, the great thing about this dish is that it can be completed in less than half an hour (unless it's by Riad's wife, then add an extra hour).

SERVES 6

Preheat the oven to 400°F.

Heat the olive oil in a medium saucepan over a low flame. Add the onion, garlic, saffron, pepper flakes, and 1 teaspoon of salt. Cook until the onions are soft and translucent, about 15 minutes. Add the tomatoes and ½ cup of water. Simmer for 20 minutes. Pass through a food mill and set aside.

Pat the fillets dry with a paper towel and season the flesh side with the remaining teaspoon of salt and a few grindings of white pepper. In a large, nonstick sauté pan, heat 2 tablespoons of the vegetable oil over a high flame until it smokes. Shake the pan with one hand while adding 3 of the fillets, skin side down,

with the other. Shake the pan again to thinly distribute the oil. Cook the fish for 3 minutes on the skin side (if the fillets begin to curl upward, press down lightly with a spatula), and 2 minutes more on the other side. Transfer to a baking sheet and hold in the oven while the other 3 fillets are cooked. Transfer the second batch to the oven and hold all the fish there while preparing the rest of the dish, which should take about 2 minutes.

Add the basil to the Fennel Confit and heat in a small saucepan. Divide the reserved tomato mixture into 6 bowls, and add a spoonful of the Fennel Confit to each. Top with the striped bass fillets and serve immediately.

INGREDIENTS

4 tablespoons olive oil
1 onion, peeled and thinly sliced
2 garlic cloves, peeled and thinly sliced
1 packed teaspoon saffron
   Pinch of red pepper flakes
2 teaspoons salt
5 beefsteak tomatoes, cored, seeded, and roughly chopped
   (see page 244)

6 striped bass fillets, about 6 ounces each
   Freshly ground white pepper
4 tablespoons vegetable oil
3 tablespoons basil, cut into thin ribbons
2 cups Fennel Confit
   (page 243)

BLACK BASS WITH CORN

AND CARAMELIZED ONIONS

Summer corn is best enjoyed when sautéed. The sweet kernels stay crisp and burst in the mouth. The black bass in this recipe, when tossed with roasted bell peppers and cilantro, is a complete dish in itself. If there aren't any roasted peppers on hand, substitute quartered cherry tomatoes.

SERVES 6

In a large skillet, heat 3 tablespoons of the olive oil over a medium flame. Add the onions and sauté until they begin to brown, about 10 minutes. Add 2 tablespoons of the butter, reduce the flame to low, and continue to cook until the onions are soft and golden brown; this can take up to 1 hour. Season with ½ teaspoon salt and set aside in a large bowl with the roasted peppers.

Preheat the oven to 200°F.

In the same skillet, heat 2 tablespoons of the olive oil and 1 tablespoon of the butter over a high flame. When the oil begins to smoke, add the corn kernels, and toss in the hot oil for 3 minutes. Taste the corn to check for doneness; depending on the variety (how tender the kernels are to begin with), more cooking time may be needed. Add the corn to the caramelized onions and roasted red peppers and toss well to combine. Season with ½ teaspoon

of salt and ¼ teaspoon of pepper. Return the mixture to the skillet.

Heat a large nonstick or cast-iron pan over a medium-high flame. Season the black bass fillets with ¼ teaspoon salt and a few grindings of pepper on both sides. Add the remaining 3 tablespoons of oil to the pan, and when it begins to smoke, add 3 of the fillets. Cook for 4 minutes on the first side, turn, and cook the second side for 3 minutes, until the fish is white and just beginning to flake. Hold the finished fillets in the oven while the remaining fish are cooked.

Warm the corn and caramelized onions over a low flame. Just before serving add the chopped cilantro and toss to combine.

To serve, lay each fillet over several spoonfuls of the warm corn and pepper mixture.

INGREDIENTS

½ cup olive oil

2 medium yellow onions, peeled and thinly sliced

3 tablespoons unsalted butter

1¼ teaspoons salt

3 roasted red peppers *(see page 249)*, sliced into ½-inch strips

10 ears corn, kernels removed from the cob *(see Note)*

6 black bass fillets, about 6 ounces each

Freshly ground black pepper

2 tablespoons chopped cilantro

REMOVING CORN FROM THE COB

Remove kernels from cobs in the following way: After shucking the corn, rub the ear with a dry towel to remove all silk strands. Use a deep bowl and stand the cob in the center with one hand and run the blade of a sharp chef's knife from top to bottom to remove the kernels. Don't cut too deeply, or you'll end up with some of the toughness from the cob.

GRILLED TUNA

WITH BLOOD ORANGE AND FENNEL

Blood oranges, typically seen around New Year's, spruce up this classic tuna salad. When fennel is added, the combination of raw and cooked is both delicious and refreshing.

SERVES 6

Combine the blood orange juice, vinegar, and sugar in a small saucepan. Simmer over a medium flame until the liquid reduces by more than half and has a thick, syrupy consistency, about 15 minutes.

Using a mandoline or sharp knife, shave the fennel into paper-thin slices. Squeeze the lemon over the sliced fennel and toss.

Start to heat the Fennel Confit in a medium saucepan over a low flame. It should be served warm, not hot.

Season the tuna steaks with 1 teaspoon of the salt and a few turns of the pepper mill. Rub the steaks with 2 tablespoons of the olive oil to prevent them from stick-

ing. Grill over medium-hot coals or in a preheated grill pan for about 4 minutes per side; a good sear should develop before turning the steaks over.

Add the basil to the shaved fennel along with the remaining tablespoon of extra-virgin olive oil, ¼ teaspoon of salt, ¼ teaspoon of white pepper, and the fresh blood orange segments.

To serve, place a few tablespoons of Fennel Confit on each plate. Top with a seared tuna steak and then drizzle the blood orange reduction over the fish. Garnish with the fresh fennel and blood orange salad.

INGREDIENTS

Juice of 2 blood oranges (at least ½ cup), plus 2 additional blood oranges, cut into segments *(see Note)*
1 tablespoon white wine vinegar
1 tablespoon sugar
1 large fennel bulb
½ lemon
2 cups Fennel Confit *(page 243)*

6 tuna steaks, about 6 ounces each, about 1½ inches thick
1¼ teaspoons sea salt
Freshly ground white pepper
3 tablespoons extra-virgin olive oil
2 tablespoons chopped fresh basil

BLOOD ORANGES

To cut an orange into segments begin by slicing off its bottom and top. Stand the orange on a cutting board and slice the peel away, from top to bottom, all the way around. This also removes the outer membrane of the segments. Then, with the orange in one hand, cut in alongside each of the membranes and remove clean segments. Do this over a bowl to capture all the juice.

TURBOT

WITH MORELS AND ASPARAGUS

Every restaurant and every green-market shopper has a favorite way to serve asparagus and morels. These ingredients mark the official start of spring. And to celebrate we add the esteemed turbot. With its firm and robust flesh, this odd-shaped fish has also inspired a special oval-shaped pot for cooking (the *turbotière*).

SERVES 6

Heat 2 tablespoons of the olive oil in a large sauté pan over a medium flame. Add half of the asparagus pieces and sauté for 5 minutes, then remove to a bowl. Sauté the remaining asparagus, remove to the bowl, and set aside.

Remove the stems from the morels. If a few are significantly larger than the others, cut them in half. Fill a bowl with cold water, drop the mushrooms in to rinse, and then gently press them between paper towels to remove the water.

Combine the port and the sherry in a small saucepan. Simmer over a medium flame until only ½ cup remains, about 15 minutes. Add the cream and simmer for 5 minutes. Set aside.

Preheat the oven to 400°F.

Heat 2 tablespoons of the olive oil in the large sauté pan until it smokes. Add the morels, ½ teaspoon of the salt, and 1 cup of water. Bring to a simmer and cook for

5 minutes. Remove the morels with a slotted spoon and transfer them to the port–sherry–cream mixture. Simmer over a low flame for 3 to 4 minutes, then remove from the heat and set aside.

Wipe the sauté pan clean with a paper towel, and add 2 tablespoons of olive oil. While that heats to the smoking point, season both sides of the turbot with salt and a few grindings of freshly ground white pepper. Add 2 or 3 fillets, depending on the size of the pan, and cook each side for 3 minutes (the fish will be slightly undercooked but will finish in the oven). Transfer the fillets onto a baking sheet and hold in the oven while sautéing the remaining fillets in the remaining 2 tablespoons of oil.

Add the chopped thyme to the morel sauce and warm over a low flame for about 5 minutes. Plate the turbot with asparagus on top and the sauce spooned over and around.

INGREDIENTS

½ cup olive oil

18 medium asparagus, peeled, woody bottoms removed, and cut on the bias into 3-inch pieces

12 ounces fresh morels

½ cup port

1 cup dry sherry

1 cup heavy cream
Salt

6 turbot fillets, about 7 ounces each
Freshly ground white pepper

1 teaspoon chopped thyme (about 10 sprigs)

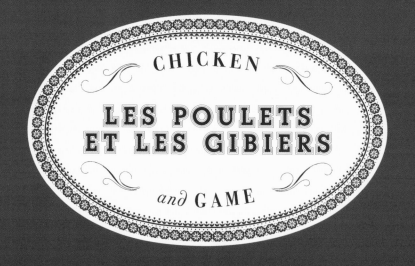

CHICKEN

LES POULETS ET LES GIBIERS

and GAME

ROAST CHICKEN FOR TWO

This dish has a devoted following and is a favorite among regulars who don't bother to look at a menu before ordering. In the restaurant, the chicken is served with Garlic Mashed Potatoes *(page 173)* and a selection of Pan-Roasted Root Vegetables *(page 198)*. At home we suggest throwing in some diced vegetables—like carrots, celery root, and mushrooms—along with the chicken, making it a very simple supper.

SERVES 2

INGREDIENTS

3 sprigs of rosemary, finely chopped

6 sprigs of thyme, finely chopped

8 sprigs of flat-leaf parsley, finely chopped

4 tablespoons (½ stick) butter, at room temperature

⅛ teaspoon plus ½ teaspoon salt

⅛ teaspoon plus ¼ teaspoon freshly ground black pepper

1 3½-pound chicken, rinsed and dried, wings snipped at the elbow

1 head of garlic, split horizontally

3 tablespoons olive oil
Roast Chicken Jus *(page 232)*, warm, optional

Preheat the oven to 450°F.

In a small bowl, combine half the rosemary, thyme, and parsley with the softened butter, using a fork to blend the herbs and butter. Season with ⅛ teaspoon of the salt and ⅛ teaspoon of the pepper. Going through the neck opening, slide the herbed butter under the skin of both breasts. Stuff the cavity with the remaining chopped herbs and the garlic. Truss the chicken with butcher's twine *(see Note)* and season with ½ teaspoon of salt and ¼ teaspoon of pepper.

Over a high flame, heat the olive oil in a heavy ovenproof sauté pan (or, if making 2 chickens, a roasting pan) until it smokes. Place the bird on its side, searing the leg and breast. Leave it untouched in the pan for at least 4 minutes, turning only when the bird is burnished brown.

Turn to brown the other breast side, and then the top and bottom of the bird so that it is well-browned on all sides.

(Note: If including diced vegetables in the pan for a one-pot meal, lower the flame to medium and add the vegetables to the pan now. Stir to coat with the olive oil and rendered chicken fat. Brown and soften the vegetables, about 10 minutes, then continue with the directions below.)

Spoon out the excess fat and transfer the pan to the oven. Cook for 40 minutes, basting occasionally. The bird is done when it reaches an internal temperature of 155°F. or when the juices run clear from the joint between leg and thigh. If the bird's skin begins to burn, cover with an aluminum-foil tent for the remainder of the cooking time.

Serve with the jus passed on the side.

TRUSSING A CHICKEN

To hold its shape and allow for even stovetop browning, it's important to properly truss the bird. Its upper wings are held tight against the body and the legs are crossed and bound at what would be the ankles. Begin by rinsing and drying the chicken, and then snipping the wings off at the elbow joint; discard or freeze the wing tips to make a stock. Lay a piece of kitchen twine, about 36 inches long, across a cutting board and place the chicken in the middle of the string. Pull the string up on both sides so that it draws the wings up against the bird's body. Bring each side of the string down along the breasts and pull snugly so the string tucks between the breast and the leg on each side. Wrap each piece of the string around the opposite ankle, then pull the string taut so the ankles are crossed and closed over the cavity. Tie the string very tightly and snip off any excess. The bird should now be snug, tight, and roundish.

CHICKEN RIESLING

This Alsatian classic is a product of the region's sweet and flowery wines. As with many French stews, pearl onions and white mushrooms garnish the dish. Browning the chicken pieces and finishing them in the oven prevents the bird from drying out, with the legs and thighs needing more cooking time than the breasts. We serve it with crispy Spaetzle *(page 194)*, but alternatives to soak up the creamy sauce could be white rice, buttered egg noodles, or even steamed potatoes.

SERVES 6

Bring a medium saucepan of salted water to a boil. Add the pearl onions and cook for 10 minutes. Drain and set aside.

Over a high flame, heat 3 tablespoons of the vegetable oil in a large Dutch oven. Add the mushrooms and sauté until they're soft and brown, about 5 minutes. Reduce the heat and add the leek and ¼ teaspoon of salt. Cook for 5 minutes, stirring frequently, until soft but not brown.

Add the wine and bring to a boil. Reduce the liquid by slightly more than half, about 12 to 15 minutes. Add the chicken jus and the blanched pearl onions and simmer for 20 minutes. Stir in the cream and keep at a low simmer.

Preheat the oven to a whopping 450°F. Season the chicken pieces with the remaining 1 teaspoon of salt and ½ teaspoon of black pepper. Heat the remaining 2 tablespoons of vegetable oil in a

large ovenproof sauté pan over a medium-high flame. When the oil begins to smoke, add the legs and thighs to the pan, skin side down. Brown for 10 minutes, forming a golden crust. Transfer the pan to the oven. Turn the pieces after 5 minutes, and cook for 5 minutes more. Place the chicken pieces, skin side up, in the simmering sauce.

Now add the breasts, skin side down, to the large sauté pan, which will be quite hot. Brown the breasts for 5 minutes on each side, then transfer to the oven for 10 minutes (no need to turn them over). Remove from the oven and add the breasts to the sauce. Turn off the flame and add a few grindings of pepper, the parsley, and the thyme. Serve in large bowls with Spaetzle, egg noodles, or rice. If preparing the Spaetzle, give the pan a quick wipe with a paper towel and use it to sauté the dumplings.

INGREDIENTS

10 ounces pearl onions, peeled

5 tablespoons vegetable oil

12 ounces white button mushrooms, quartered

1 leek, white part only, split, cut into ½-inch slices, and rinsed well *(see page 144)*

1¼ teaspoons salt

2 cups Riesling wine

2 cups Roast Chicken Jus *(page 232)*

½ cup heavy cream

2 3-pound chickens, each cut into 6 pieces (legs, thighs, and breasts)

½ teaspoon freshly ground black pepper, plus more to taste

2 tablespoons chopped flat-leaf parsley

2 sprigs of thyme, leaves only

COQ AU VIN

Though currently synonymous with chicken, Coq au Vin was originally made by braising the meat from a sinewy old rooster in a cheap red wine for a long period of time.

SERVES 4

In a large bowl, combine the legs, onion, carrot, celery, garlic, wine, and bouquet garni. Cover with plastic wrap and refrigerate for 24 to 36 hours.

Strain the legs and the vegetables from the marinade, reserving the liquid, and separating the legs and vegetables. Season the legs with salt and pepper.

Heat the olive oil in a large Dutch oven. When it begins to smoke, add the legs in batches, being sure not to crowd the pan. Brown evenly and deeply on all sides, about 8 minutes per side. Set the finished legs to the side and discard the oil; replenish it between batches.

When finished browning the legs, reduce heat to medium and add the reserved vegetables to the pot. Cook until they soften and begin to brown, about 5 to 8 minutes. Stir in the tomato paste and cook for about 2 minutes, and then add the flour, stirring again for about 2 minutes. Add the reserved wine marinade and, as it bubbles up, use a wooden spoon to scrape the bottom of the pot and incorporate any flavorful bits into the broth. Reduce the liquid by half, about 20 to 25 minutes, and then add the stock. As it reaches a

boil, reduce the flame to low and maintain a slow and gentle simmer for 1 hour, at which point the meat should be meltingly tender.

Meanwhile, prepare the rest of the ingredients: Blanche the pearl onions in boiling water for 5 to 7 minutes, until tender. Strain and set aside. Cook the bacon in a dry sauté pan over medium heat until brown, about 10 minutes, and remove with a slotted spoon. Add the mushrooms to the sauté pan and the now very hot rendered bacon fat, cook until brown, about 5 minutes, and remove with a slotted spoon. Add the blanched pearl onions to the pan, sautéing until they too are brown, about 5 minutes.

Remove the legs from the braising liquid and strain the contents of the pot, reserving the liquid and discarding the vegetables. Bring to a strong simmer and skim the surface of the sauce as it bubbles, removing any visible fat. When the sauce has reduced by half, return the legs to the pot along with the bacon, onions, and mushrooms and simmer for an additional 15 minutes. Just prior to serving, add the chopped parsley.

INGREDIENTS

4 large stewing hen legs

1 large yellow onion, cut into ½-inch dice

1 large carrot, cut into ½-inch dice

2 celery stalks, cut into medium dice

1 head of garlic, halved horizontally

1 bottle red wine

1 bouquet garni (see page 31)

Salt and freshly ground black pepper to taste

¼ cup olive oil

2 tablespoons tomato paste

3 tablespoons all-purpose flour

3 cups Veal Stock (page 231)

1 pint pearl onions, peeled

½ pound smoked slab bacon, diced

1 pound small domestic mushrooms

3 tablespoons chopped flat-leaf parsley

DUCK CONFIT

Confit is an ancient method of preserving: The meat is first salted, then cooked, and finally stored in a great amount of fat, where it can remain in a sort of suspended animation for months on end.

Today confit is no longer driven by necessity but rather by a desire to always have a little duck meat in the fridge. The legs, crisped in a hot pan before serving, are savory and robust, and the meat pulls away from the bone in delicious slivers.

Classic uses include Cassoulet *(page 120)*, *garbure* (a thick cabbage soup), and cold salads. We serve it simply, with frisée and Pommes à la Sarladaise *(page 178)*.

***

SERVES 6

Using a pan large enough to hold the duck legs in a single layer (a rectangular casserole dish works well), spread half the rosemary, half the thyme, and 1 garlic head in the pan. Salt both sides of the duck legs and lay them, skin side down, over the herbs. Sprinkle the pepper over the legs, then place half a cinnamon stick, half a star anise, and half a bay leaf on top of each leg. Arrange the remaining herbs and garlic on top. Cover with plastic wrap and refrigerate for 36 hours.

INGREDIENTS

- 4 sprigs of rosemary, cut into 1-inch pieces
- 6 sprigs of thyme, cut into 1-inch pieces
- 2 heads of garlic, unpeeled, lightly crushed with a mallet
- 6 tablespoons kosher salt
- 6 Moulard duck legs (about 2½ to 3 pounds), excess flaps of fat removed
- 1 tablespoon freshly ground black pepper
- 3 cinnamon sticks, each snapped in half
- 3 star anise, each broken in half
- 3 bay leaves, each broken into 2 pieces
- 4 pounds rendered duck fat

Preheat the oven to 225°F.

Brush the salt and herbs off the duck legs. Over a low flame, melt the duck fat in a large saucepan or Dutch oven. Add the duck legs to the melted fat and bring to a very low simmer. Cover the pot with a tight-fitting lid and transfer to the middle shelf of the oven. Cook for 3 hours.

Remove the legs and strain the fat through a fine sieve to remove any solids. Put the duck legs in the container in which they'll be stored and add the strained fat. Make sure the legs are covered by at least 1 inch of fat. Storing in groups of 2 or 3 legs is sometimes more convenient for serving later, as well as more space efficient. Cool and store the containers in the refrigerator.

When it's time to eat the duck legs, remove the container from the fridge, and set it in some gently simmering water to melt the fat and loosen the legs. Remove the legs from the melted fat and set aside. (If serving with Pommes à la Sarladaise, some of the duck fat will be used for the preparation of the potatoes, so set aside, and indeed save for future use, such as for excellent hash browns.)

Take 2 tablespoons of the duck fat and add to a sauté pan. Over a medium flame, let the fat get very hot and then add the legs, skin side down. Cook for 4 to 5 minutes, browning the skin well. Turn to briefly sauté the other side, 3 to 4 minutes. Serve with Pommes à la Sarladaise and lightly dressed frisée.

DUCK CONFIT

The meaty legs of the Moulard duck are shapely and succulent, which is why they're preferred to the lesser gams of other ducks. The traditional way of storing duck confit is in glazed earthenware pots. Handy alternatives are large Pyrex measuring cups or covered casseroles. Plastic containers, which can impart an unpleasant taste, are not recommended. Be sure that the legs are completely covered with fat before storing in the refrigerator. (Duck legs and rendered duck fat can be ordered by calling 1-800-DAR-TAGN or on-line at www.dartagnan.com.)

DUCK À L'ORANGE

This classic dish displays all the talents of the saucier, a position normally reserved for the most qualified cook in the kitchen. Duck à l'Orange brings out his talents to combine three distinctly different flavors.

Prepare the sauce ahead of time: Melt 2 tablespoons of the butter in a sauté pan over medium heat. Continue to heat after the foam subsides, swirling the pan a bit, until the butter becomes brown and frothy, about 1 minute. Add the shallot, garlic, thyme, peppercorns, and cloves. Stir to combine, and then sauté until the shallots begin to brown, about 2 minutes. Add the honey and continue to cook for 3 to 5 minutes, during which time the contents of the pan will take on a rich caramel color. Carefully add the vinegar to stop further caramelization (the pan will spatter a bit). Add the Grand Marnier, fresh orange juice, and the grated zest. Raise the flame to high and reduce the contents of the pan by about two thirds, to a syrupy glaze, about 10 minutes. Add the stock and bring to a simmer. Skim off any fat or impurities that rise to the surface, and again, reduce the contents of the pan, this time by a third, or until the sauce is rich in consistency, about 10 to 12 minutes. Strain and reserve until ready to use. (Cool and refrigerate if making in advance.)

INGREDIENTS

4 tablespoons unsalted butter

1 shallot, peeled and thinly sliced

1 garlic clove, peeled and thinly sliced

2 sprigs of thyme

1/4 teaspoon cracked black peppercorns

2 whole cloves

1/4 cup honey

1/4 cup sherry vinegar

1/2 cup Grand Marnier or Cointreau

Juice of 3 oranges (about 1/2 cup)

1/4 teaspoon freshly grated orange zest

1 cup Veal Stock *(page 231)* or Roast Chicken Jus *(page 232)*

3 oranges

1/2 cup sugar

6 duck breasts (Long Island or Muscovy, about 3 pounds)

1 teaspoon salt

1/2 teaspoon freshly ground black pepper

Preheat the oven to 425°F.

Now prepare the confit orange zest: Zest the 3 whole oranges by slicing off the zest in thin strips, being careful to leave the bitter pith behind. Then chop the strips into long, thin matchsticks. Take the fruits of your labor and blanch in a pot of boiling water for 5 minutes. Strain through a fine-mesh sieve. Combine the sugar with 1 cup of water in a saucepan. Add the blanched orange zest, bring to a gentle simmer, and cook for 20 minutes. Strain and reserve the zest.

Heat a large sauté pan over a medium-high flame. Score the skin of the duck breasts in a criss-cross pattern, cutting in about $\frac{1}{8}$ inch. Season the breasts with the salt and pepper, and add 3 breasts to the dry pan, skin side down. Sear for 4 to 5 minutes, until a crisp brown skin has developed. Remove the seared breasts to a plate, pour off the rendered fat, and add the remaining 3 breasts to the pan. Sear them in the same fashion. When finished, return the first batch to the pan and slide them all into the oven, browned sides up. Cook for 6 to 7 minutes for a nice medium-rare, or 10 minutes for medium.

Bring the sauce to a simmer. Whisk in the remaining 2 tablespoons of butter just before serving. Plate the breasts and drizzle with the sauce and confit orange zest.

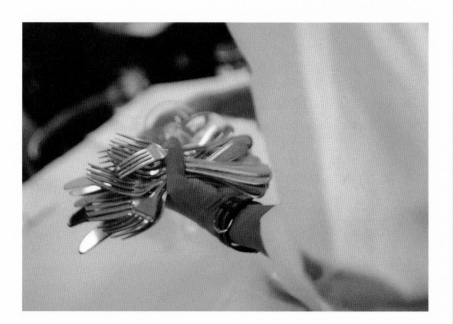

DUCK SHEPHERD'S PIE

This is also known as Hachis Parmentier, named for the decorated French army officer Antoine Parmentier, who was an indefatigable advocate of the potato. In this version braised duck, veal stock, and earthy root vegetables occupy the roles usually held by last night's leftovers. While it may seem more strenuous to prepare than the traditional pub version, the results are worth it. And it's all the better if made in advance.

Use six round individual gratin dishes (5¾-inch diameter) or one 15 × 10-inch casserole.

SERVES 6

INGREDIENTS

8 Moulard duck legs (about 3½ pounds), excess fat trimmed

2 bottles cabernet sauvignon

2 carrots, cut into ½-inch dice (about 1 cup)

3 celery stalks, cut into ½-inch dice (about 1 cup)

1 large yellow onion, cut into ½-inch dice (about 1½ cups)

3 sprigs of thyme

1 bay leaf

1 head of garlic, halved horizontally, plus 4 garlic cloves, minced

1½ teaspoons salt, plus more to taste

Freshly ground black pepper

2 tablespoons vegetable oil

2 tablespoons tomato paste

3 tablespoons all-purpose flour

4 cups Veal Stock *(page 231)* or Chicken Stock *(page 230)*

7 medium Yukon gold potatoes, peeled and cut into 2-inch pieces

3 parsnips, peeled and cut into 2-inch pieces

2 celery roots, peeled and cut into 2-inch pieces

¼ cup heavy cream

2 tablespoons unsalted butter

3 to 4 tablespoons grated Parmesan cheese

In a large bowl, combine the duck legs, wine, carrots, celery, onion, thyme, bay leaf, and the halved head of garlic. Cover with plastic wrap and marinate in the refrigerator overnight.

The next day, strain out the duck legs and the vegetables, and reserve the marinade. Separate the legs from the vegetables. Season the duck legs with the salt and a few grindings of black pepper. In a large Dutch oven, heat 1 tablespoon of the vegetable oil over a high flame, until it smokes. Working in batches, brown the duck legs starting with the skin side down, about 5 minutes per side. They'll render a lot of fat, so spoon out the excess as necessary. Hold the browned duck legs aside. If any burnt spots have developed on the bottom of the pan, scrape them away with a wooden spoon to prevent them from turning the dish bitter.

Wipe the Dutch oven clean with a paper towel and add a fresh tablespoon of vegetable oil. Over a medium flame, add the reserved carrots, celery, onion, and minced garlic. Sauté until brown, about 5 minutes. Stir in the tomato paste until it melts away, then stir in the flour. Raise the heat to high and add the reserved marinade. Bring to a boil and reduce the liquid by half, about 30 minutes.

Return the duck legs to the pot, add the stock, and, again, bring to a boil. Cover the pot with a tight-fitting lid and cook either in a 375°F. oven or on top of the stove at a low simmer. Cook for 3 hours, or until the meat is very tender and falling off the bone.

Meanwhile, prepare the root vegetables: Put the peeled and cut potatoes, parsnips, and celery roots in a large saucepan and cover with cold salted water. Bring to a boil and cook until tender, about 25 minutes. Strain and pass the vegetables through a food mill (or mash them by hand). Stir in the cream and butter. Season to taste with salt and pepper, cover with foil, and set aside.

When the duck is finished cooking, remove the legs from the pot and strain the cooking liquid into a large saucepan. Reserve the solids, but remove and discard the bay leaf, thyme sprigs, and garlic remnants. Skim the fat from the surface of the sauce using a ladle or a defatter. Set the saucepan over a high flame and reduce the liquid by half, continuing to skim as necessary, about 30 to 45 minutes. There should be approximately 3 cups of sauce.

Preheat the oven to 350°F.

When the duck legs are cool enough to handle, remove the fatty skin and pull the meat from the bones. Discard all excess fat and place the clean bits of meat in a large bowl. Fold in the reserved diced carrots, celery, and onion, and pour in just enough of the sauce (about 1½ cups) to loosely bind the meat and vegetables. Spoon the duck mixture into the gratin dishes and spread the mashed root vegetables over the top, about ¾ inch high, leaving a ¼-inch border. Sprinkle with grated Parmesan cheese and bake for 30 minutes. Run under a broiler for 2 minutes to form a golden brown crust.

PRE-PREPARATION

The potato mixture will spread smoothest if all the components have cooled completely. The pies can be assembled, covered with foil, and held in the fridge to be baked the next day. This produces both the best results and an unusually clean kitchen for guests.

CASSOULET

A classic winter dinner from the Gascony region, Cassoulet is a French national dish over which endless debates have raged regarding recipes, methods, and origins. This version includes duck confit and pork belly. The Cassoulet we prepare at the restaurant takes six days from start to finish and includes pig knuckles and pork confit. This recipe is somewhat abbreviated, taking just three days and a significantly smaller pot.

SERVES 6

DAY 1 Cure the pork belly: In a large casserole dish or deep bowl, cover the pork belly in the salt. Refrigerate overnight.

DAY 2 Soak the beans: Pick through the beans and discard any pebbles or discolored ones. Pour them into a large bowl, cover with water, and soak overnight.

Remove the pork belly from the refrigerator and rinse away the salt. Return the meat to the casserole dish and add the head of garlic, cloves, bay leaves, thyme, rosemary, and peppercorns. Cover with

INGREDIENTS

- 1 pound fresh pork belly
- 2 cups kosher salt
- 2 pounds Tarbais beans *(see Note)*
- 1 head of garlic, halved horizontally
- 4 whole cloves
- 2 bay leaves
- 8 sprigs of thyme
- 6 sprigs of rosemary
- 1 tablespoon whole black peppercorns
- ½ cup duck fat
- 1 large yellow onion, diced (about 2 cups)
- 3 large carrots, diced (about 2 cups)

- 6 celery stalks, diced (about 2 cups)
- ½ cup tomato paste
- 2 cups canned plum tomatoes, drained and chopped
- 2 cloves plus 2 tablespoons garlic, minced
- 1 bouquet garni *(see page 31)*
- 6 cups Chicken Stock *(page 230)*
- 1 pound garlic sausage, each cut in half
- 6 confit duck legs *(see page 111)*, browned
- 1 cup bread crumbs
- ¼ cup chopped flat-leaf parsley

plastic wrap and allow the flavors to intermingle overnight.

DAY 3 Assemble and cook the cassoulet: Remove the pork belly from the refrigerator and cut into 1-inch cubes. Add the herbs and spices to the bouquet garni. Discard the garlic.

Preheat the oven to 350°F. Drain the beans.

In a large ovenproof casserole or Dutch oven, melt the duck fat over a medium flame. Add the diced onion and cook for 5 minutes to soften but not brown. Add the carrots and celery and continue to cook for 5 minutes more. Add the soaked beans, tomato paste, chopped tomatoes, 2 cloves minced garlic, bouquet garni, and the pork belly. Stir well to combine. Add the stock and bring to a simmer. Skim away any foam that accumulates on the surface, cover, and transfer to the oven. Cook for 2 hours, at which point the beans should be tender. Remove the casserole from the oven and add the sausage pieces and the duck confit. Stir gently to combine.

Combine the bread crumbs, 2 tablespoons minced garlic, and chopped parsley in a small bowl. Mix thoroughly and sprinkle over the casserole. Return uncovered to the oven and bake for 30 minutes, until the crumbly top browns, bubbles, and looks delicious.

WHITE BEANS

The white beans of the Tarbais region have begun to show up at markets around this country. Seek them out for their fat and creamy texture; they are the soul of the dish. If they are not available, go for Carelli or Great Northerns.

ROAST SQUAB WITH GIBLETS

The success of this dish may well depend on the quality of your roasting pan. At the restaurant, we use heavy sauté pans that slide into the oven after the birds have been seared. (Make sure the pan has a flat bottom, not one designed to drain fat away from the center, which will cause burning.) The squabs are boned and then "frogged," or prepared *en crapaudine*, that is, flattened to allow for even cooking and ease of serving. This is a fairly easy dish to master and a pleasure to eat, especially with soft Mascarpone-Parmesan Polenta *(page 185)*.

SERVES 6

Bring the Roast Chicken Jus to a boil in a small saucepan. Reduce the liquid by a third. Set aside.

Preheat the oven to 375°F.

Melt 2 tablespoons of the butter in a sauté pan. When the foam subsides, add the shallots and garlic and cook over a medium flame for 5 minutes, or until they're soft and translucent but not brown. Set aside.

Season the squabs with ½ teaspoon of salt and a few turns of the pepper mill. Heat a large roasting pan on top of the stove using 2 burners set over medium-high flames. Add the olive oil. When it starts to smoke, add the squabs, skin side down. Cook for 3 to 4 minutes, or until the skin is crisp and brown. Add 4 tablespoons of butter to the pan along with the thyme and sage. Baste the birds with the foaming butter and transfer the pan to the oven. Roast the squab for 5 minutes, basting once, before turning and continuing to cook for 2 minutes more for a pink and juicy result.

Meanwhile, bring the chicken jus just to a boil in a small saucepan. Add the shallots, pancetta, livers, and squab giblets and cook just until it comes back to a simmer. Stir in the remaining 1 tablespoon of butter. Keep warm over low heat.

When the squabs have finished cooking, let them rest for 5 minutes. Add chopped parsley just before serving.

INGREDIENTS

2 cups Roast Chicken Jus
  (page 232)

7 tablespoons unsalted butter

3 shallots, minced (about
  3 tablespoons)

1 garlic clove, minced

6 squabs, backbone removed,
  breast snipped at the
  wishbone by the butcher,
  giblets reserved and finely
  diced

½ teaspoon salt
  Freshly ground black
  pepper

¼ cup olive oil

4 sprigs of thyme

2 sprigs of sage

¼ pound pancetta, minced

2 chicken livers, minced

1 bunch of flat-leaf parsley,
  roughly chopped

GRILLED QUAIL

WITH BRAISED FIGS AND PORT GLAZE

Quail is the kind of thing that you start eating with the good silver and finish with your fingers. While the birds are widely available deboned, the leg bones remain as tiny drumsticks. They cook quickly and should be eaten at a succulent medium-rare.

SERVES 6

Lay out a slice of prosciutto with a fresh sage leaf on top. Place a half quail at the narrow end of the prosciutto slice and wrap tightly. Repeat the process until all the quail are wrapped. Season the little packages with ¼ teaspoon salt and a few grindings of freshly ground black pepper. Set aside in the refrigerator until ready to grill.

Set a large saucepan of salted water over a high flame. When the water comes to a boil, add the fingerlings and cook until tender, about 15 minutes; they should offer little to no resistance when pierced with a fork. Drain and set aside until cool enough to handle, then remove the skins (by hand or with a paring knife) and set them aside to be sautéed later.

Heat 3 tablespoons of the olive oil and 1 tablespoon of the butter in a sauté pan. Add the asparagus and sauté over medium heat until tender and slightly brown, about 8 minutes. Set aside on a plate.

Place the port, cinnamon stick, peppercorns, cloves, bay leaf, and star anise in a small saucepan. Bring to a boil over a high flame and reduce the liquid by a third, about 10 minutes. Reduce the heat to low and add the figs. Gently braise them for 10 minutes, until plump and tender. Remove from the heat. Carefully transfer the figs to a plate and reduce the port by a third, about 5 minutes. Swirl in 2 tablespoons of butter, return the figs to the pot, and set aside.

Again in the sauté pan, heat 3 tablespoons of the olive oil with the remaining tablespoon of butter over a medium flame. When the foam subsides, add the reserved fingerlings, toss gently to coat, and sauté for 7 to 10 minutes, until brown. Add the reserved asparagus and sauté for an additional 5 minutes. Season with ½ teaspoon of salt and ¼ teaspoon of pepper.

Rub the remaining 2 tablespoons of olive oil over the prosciutto-wrapped quail. Over a hot grill or in a preheated broiler, grill the wrapped quail for 3 minutes per side for a rosy pink interior (as we prefer them), or 4 to 5 minutes per side for medium.

Put two quail halves on each plate. Serve with the sautéed asparagus and fingerling potatoes, and garnish with the warm braised figs and a drizzle of the port glaze. Sprinkle with a bit of the chopped parsley.

INGREDIENTS

24 thin slices of prosciutto
1 bunch of fresh sage
12 boneless quail, split lengthwise, along the back
Salt
Freshly ground black pepper
1 pound fingerling potatoes
½ cup olive oil
4 tablespoons unsalted butter
1 pound asparagus, bottoms trimmed and peeled, cut on the bias into 2-inch pieces

1½ cups port
1 cinnamon stick
6 whole black peppercorns
3 whole cloves
1 bay leaf
3 star anise pods
12 fresh figs
1 bunch of flat-leaf parsley, roughly chopped

RABBIT MOUTARDE

For this classic braised stew we use only the legs, rather than the whole rabbit. They turn the most stunning and even shade of brown in the pan, giving the cook a strong sense of accomplishment at the stove. Serve with buttered egg noodles or Spaetzle *(page 194)*.

SERVES 6

Combine the rabbit legs, wine, onion, carrots, celery, garlic, and thyme in a nonreactive bowl. Cover with plastic wrap and refrigerate overnight. The next day, remove the legs from the marinade and strain the vegetables from the wine, catching the wine in a bowl. Pat the legs dry with paper towels and season with 1 teaspoon of salt and a few grindings of white pepper.

Heat 3 tablespoons of the vegetable oil in a large Dutch oven over a high flame. When it's very hot, add the mushrooms. Sauté for 5 minutes, or until the mushrooms are nicely browned. Season them with a pinch of salt, and then remove from the pot and set aside.

Replenish the pan with 3 tablespoons of oil and heat over a high flame until it smokes. Add half the rabbit and brown well all around. Remove to a bowl, discard the fat, and add ½ cup of the stock. Bring to a rolling boil and use a wooden spoon to scrape the meat drippings from the bottom of the pan. When thoroughly scraped clean, pour the stock over the cooked and reserved legs, and give the pot a quick wipe with a paper towel.

Again, add 3 tablespoons of vegetable oil to the pot, heat over a high flame, and when it smokes, add the remaining rabbit legs. When they're well browned, add them to the bowl with the first batch of legs, and do away with the fat in the pan. Reduce the flame to medium and add the butter. When it's melted, add the reserved marinated vegetables, and cook for 5 minutes, lightly browning them. Add the flour, stirring until it disappears, and then the reserved wine marinade. Raise the flame to high, bring the liquid to a boil, and reduce by half, about 10 minutes. Add the rabbit legs along with the pan drippings and the remaining 5 cups of Chicken Stock. Bring to a slow simmer, cover, and cook for 1½ hours.

Meanwhile, bring a small pot of salted water to a boil. Add the pearl onions and cook for 10 minutes, or until tender. Strain and add to the reserved mushrooms.

When the rabbit has finished cooking, use tongs to gently remove the legs. Strain the cooking liquid, discarding the solids and returning the liquid to the pot. Bring to a boil and reduce by half. Add the mustard and heavy cream. Simmer for 5 minutes before returning the rabbit to the pot along with the mushrooms and pearl onions. Continue to simmer for another 5 minutes to heat the mushrooms and onions. Add the chopped parsley just before serving.

INGREDIENTS

12 rabbit legs

1 bottle dry white wine (such as sauvignon blanc)

1 medium onion, diced medium

3 large carrots, diced medium (about 1 cup)

4 celery stalks, diced medium (about 1 cup)

4 garlic cloves, roughly chopped

8 sprigs of thyme

1 teaspoon salt, plus more to taste

Freshly ground white pepper

½ cup plus 1 tablespoon vegetable oil

12 ounces white mushrooms, cleaned and quartered

5½ cups Chicken Stock (*page 230*)

2 tablespoons unsalted butter

2 tablespoons all-purpose flour

12 ounces pearl onions, peeled

3 tablespoons Dijon mustard

½ cup heavy cream

¼ cup roughly chopped flat-leaf parsley

LES VIANDES

MEAT

STEAK FRITES

Steak Frites symbolizes Balthazar. It is our most popular dish and has been since day one. Those who crave meat and potatoes are always satisfied beyond their wildest dreams.

SERVES 4

To make the butter, combine all the ingredients in a bowl either with a spoon or with a standing mixer fitted with the paddle attachment. Spoon the butter onto a sheet of plastic wrap and roll into a cylinder, about 2 inches in diameter. Refrigerate until firm.

To cook the steaks, preheat the grill. Arrange the coals so that there's an area of high heat and an area of a more moderate heat. Set the grill about 3 inches above the coals. If cooking indoors, preheat a dry grill pan over a high flame for at least 3 minutes.

Season the steaks with the salt and pepper, and then rub with the olive oil. Sear the steaks on the hottest part of the grill, about 3 minutes on each side, and then move them to a more moderate heat (or lower the flame to medium if using a grill pan) to cook for an additional 3 minutes per side for medium-rare; add 2 minutes per side for medium. (If using a grill pan, reduce the cooking times—2 minutes per side for medium rare, 3 minutes per side for medium.) Let the steaks rest for 5 minutes (during which time the second blanching of the French Fries can take place). As always, an instant-read thermometer removes the guesswork, telling you exactly when the steaks reach 125°F. for medium-rare, or 130°F. for medium.

Serve with a pat of maître d'hôtel butter melting over each steak.

INGREDIENTS

FOR THE MAÎTRE D'HÔTEL BUTTER

½ pound (2 sticks) unsalted butter, softened

2 tablespoons finely chopped flat-leaf parsley

1 shallot, finely chopped

½ garlic clove, finely chopped

½ teaspoon chopped fresh sage

1 tablespoon chopped fresh chives

¼ teaspoon salt

Pinch of freshly ground white pepper

FOR THE STEAKS

4 steaks, about 10 ounces each, about 1 inch thick

2 tablespoons salt

2 tablespoons coarsely ground black pepper

3 tablespoons olive oil

French Fries *(page 170)* prepared up to the point of the first frying

STEAK AU POIVRE

Serve with French Fries *(page 170), bien sûr.*

SERVES 4

INGREDIENTS

3 tablespoons black peppercorns

3 tablespoons pink peppercorns

3 tablespoons green peppercorns

2 tablespoons coriander seeds

4 dry-aged strip steaks, about 10 ounces each, about 1½ inch thick

1½ teaspoons salt

½ cup plus 1 tablespoon peanut oil

½ pound beef scraps from butcher

6 shallots, peeled and thinly sliced

3 garlic cloves, peeled and sliced

2 tablespoons canned (brined) peppercorns

2 cups dry white wine

1 cup brandy

2 cups Veal Stock *(page 231)* or Chicken Stock *(page 230)*

¾ cup heavy cream

Coarsely grind the 3 types of whole peppercorns and coriander seeds in a spice grinder or food processor. Season the steaks on both sides with 1 teaspoon salt and then rub the ground peppercorns onto the steaks, using the palm of your hand to pat them on so that they stick. Catch the excess on a plate. Set the steaks aside.

Preheat the oven to 450°F.

Over a medium-high flame, heat 3 tablespoons of the peanut oil in a heavy-bottomed medium saucepan. When the oil smokes, add the meat scraps and brown well on all sides, about 5 minutes total. When the scraps are well browned, pour off all but 2 tablespoons of the rendered fat. Lower the flame to medium and add the shallots, garlic, brined peppercorns, and 1 teaspoon of the excess ground peppercorns. Cook, stirring frequently, for 5 minutes, or until the shallots are browned. Turn the flame off momentarily to add the wine and brandy, stir well, and then bring the liquid to a boil over a medium-high heat. Reduce by

half, about 5 to 7 minutes. Add the stock and bring to a boil, then reduce the heat to medium and maintain a simmer. Be sure to skim away any fat that accumulates on the surface. Reduce the liquid by half, about 30 minutes. When it's nearly finished reducing, bring the cream to a boil in a small saucepan and then set aside. Strain the sauce into the hot cream and keep warm over a low flame.

Preheat 2 large, heavy sauté pans over a high flame until the pans are very hot, about 3 minutes. Add 3 tablespoons of peanut oil to each pan. When it smokes, add the steaks and cook for 3 minutes per side, forming a dark and crisp coating of pepper. Transfer the pans to the oven and cook for 6 minutes for rare, 8 minutes for medium-rare (130°F. on an instant-read thermometer), or 10 minutes for medium (135° to 140°F.).

Let the steaks rest for 10 minutes before serving. Serve the steaks with several tablespoons of sauce.

DRY-AGING

The steak we serve is dry-aged, meaning that it sits, exposed, in a temperature-controlled room (slightly above freezing) while the meat's natural enzymes break down its muscle fibers. The result is a steak that's not merely tender, but that also tastes richly of beef in a way that non-aged or wet-aged beef simply doesn't. There's a premium paid for all this flavor, though, covering the costs of shelf space in a cold locker, as well as the shrinkage from evaporation. Speak with your local butcher (or visit Lobel.com or OmahaSteaks.com) to order prime dry-aged beef.

CÔTE DE BOEUF

One of our *plats pour deux*, this dish is usually ordered in waves at the restaurant. This is probably due to its dining room presentation: before slicing, the finished rib steak is sent sizzling on an oven platter ceremoniously through the dining room, which has an effect not unlike a television commercial: Suddenly everyone wants one.

For the passionate steak lover, the rib is well marbled, deeply flavorful, and expensive. It tastes best at medium-rare or medium; rare doesn't show this cut to its best advantage. For extra indulgence, melt a couple of tablespoons of butter over the steak as it comes out of the oven.

SERVES 2

Preheat the oven to 450°F.

Season both sides of the steak with the salt and pepper. Using a heavy, ovenproof skillet (cast iron is ideal), heat the vegetable oil over a high flame until it begins to smoke. Sear the steak, about 3 minutes per side, to form a brown crust.

Transfer the skillet to the oven. The steak will render a fair amount of fat as it finishes cooking in the oven, so either place a small rack (like a cooling rack for cookies) under the beef to prevent it from deep-frying, or spoon the fat out of the pan every 10 minutes or so. Turn the steak over after 15 minutes in the oven and cook for another 30 minutes—a total of 45 minutes in the oven—for medium-rare (an internal temperature of 130°F.). Allow the finished steak to rest for at least 10 minutes or as long as 30 minutes before serving.

INGREDIENTS

1 rib steak (about 3 pounds and 2¾ inches thick), at room temperature

1 teaspoon salt

1 teaspoon coarsely ground black pepper

2 tablespoons vegetable oil

BRAISED SHORT RIBS

This is our Saturday-night *plat du jour* and, because its preparation involves the basics of French cooking, it's also the first dish we teach our young cooks: There's the browning of the meat, the softening of the mirepoix, the reduction of wine, and the long braise in stock. It's a forgiving dish that calls for patience rather than precision. It's also the ideal meal to make ahead of time, as it benefits greatly from a night's rest. Serve with Garlic Mashed Potatoes *(page 173)* and Pan-Roasted Root Vegetables *(page 198)*.

SERVES 6

Preheat the oven to 325°F.

Bind each rib with cotton kitchen twine. Place the rosemary, thyme, and bay leaf between the two celery halves and bind with kitchen twine.

Season the short ribs with 2 teaspoons of the salt and the pepper. Heat the oil in a large Dutch oven over a high flame until it smokes. In two batches, brown the short ribs well on both sides, about 3 minutes per side, pouring off all but 3 tablespoons of oil between batches. Remove the ribs and set aside when done.

Lower the flame to medium, and add the carrots, onion, shallots, and garlic to the pot. Sauté for 5 minutes, until the onion is

INGREDIENTS

6 beef short ribs (5 to 7 pounds)
2 sprigs of rosemary
6 sprigs of thyme
1 bay leaf
1 celery stalk, halved
3 teaspoons kosher salt
2 teaspoons coarsely ground black pepper
3 tablespoons vegetable oil
3 medium carrots, peeled and cut into 1-inch pieces
1 medium onion, roughly chopped

4 shallots, peeled and sliced ¼ inch thick
5 garlic cloves, peeled and halved
3 tablespoons tomato paste
3 tablespoons all-purpose flour
½ cup ruby port
4 cups full-bodied red wine, such as cabernet sauvignon
6 cups Veal Stock *(page 231)*

soft and light brown. Stir in the tomato paste and cook for 2 minutes. Add the flour and stir well to combine. Add the port, red wine, and the celery–herb bundle. Raise the flame to high and cook until the liquid is reduced by a third, about 20 minutes.

Return the ribs to the pot (they will stack into two layers). Add the stock and the remaining 1 teaspoon of salt; if the stock doesn't cover the ribs by at least 1 inch, add water up to that level. Bring to a gentle simmer, cover, transfer to the preheated oven, and cook for 3 hours. Visit the pot occasionally and stir the ribs,

bringing the ones on the bottom up to the top. They're done when the meat is fork tender and falling off the bone.

Transfer the ribs to a large platter and remove the strings. Skim any fat from the surface of the sauce, and then strain through a sieve into a medium saucepan. Discard the solids. Over medium heat, bring the sauce to a strong simmer and reduce the liquid until slightly less then half (4 cups) remains, about 1 hour.

Return the ribs to the pot, simmer for 10 minutes to reheat, and serve.

BRAISING SHORT RIBS

As with all tough cuts of meat, short ribs are best when braised. A long and gentle simmer breaks down the abundant fat and connective tissue, rendering the ribs tender and velvety in texture. Veal Stock (page 231) adds its own inherent silky richness. Though canned beef stock makes a convenient substitute, the results will not be equal to homemade.

Ask the butcher to cut the ribs across the rack, as opposed to along the bone, so there are 3 short bones in every piece.

ROAST RACK OF VEAL

This majestic piece of meat is always on our New Year's Eve menu. Like all roasts, this is deceptively easy to prepare. Roasting is best done in the home kitchen, where undisturbed cooking and resting time yield the most perfect results. Serve with Pan-Roasted Root Vegetables *(page 198)* and Garlic Mashed Potatoes *(page 173)*. The veal rib roast should, like all specialty cuts of meat, be ordered a few days ahead from the butcher. Ask for a 7-rib roast (also known as a "hotel rack") bound with butcher's twine, and ask to have the bones frenched, or scraped clean of meat and fat, to add elegance to this flavorful and expensive cut. Save and freeze the trimmed scraps to prepare a Sauce Bordelaise *(page 248)* on another day.

SERVES 4 TO 6

Preheat the oven to 450°F.

Season the rack of veal with the salt and pepper.

On the stovetop, heat a large roasting pan over 2 burners set to high flames. Add the vegetable oil. When it starts to smoke, place the veal in the pan, searing the side with the most flesh first. Sear for 5 minutes and then rotate, browning as much of the surface area of the rib roast as possible.

Add the onions, carrots, garlic, thyme, and rosemary, and transfer the pan to the oven. Roast for 45 minutes, stirring the vegetables about every 10 minutes, until an instant-read thermometer reaches 130°F. Transfer the meat to a cooling rack set over a plate. Pour the contents of the roasting pan into a colander, reserving the vegetables and discarding the liquid, and set the roasting pan back on the stovetop.

Melt 2 tablespoons of the butter in a small saucepan. When the foam subsides, whisk in the flour until a smooth, pale roux forms. Set aside.

Add the Chicken Stock to the roasting pan and bring to a boil over high heat. Use a wooden spoon to scrape up the meat drippings from the bottom of the pan while the stock bubbles. Reduce the liquid by half, about 5 minutes, then whisk in the roux until a smooth gravy results. Whisk in the remaining 2 tablespoons of butter. Strain through a sieve, if you're a fastidious type, and keep hot on the stove while the rack is carved.

Slice the rack into individual ribs, knife against each bone, starting with the lean side. Serve the gravy alongside.

INGREDIENTS

1 rack of veal, 8 to 9 pounds

2 teaspoons salt

1 tablespoon coarsely ground black pepper

¼ cup vegetable oil

3 medium yellow onions, halved, each half cut into 3 wedges

8 medium carrots, peeled and cut into ½-inch bias slices

1 head of garlic, halved horizontally

15 sprigs of thyme

3 sprigs of rosemary

4 tablespoons unsalted butter

3 tablespoons all-purpose flour

4 cups Chicken Stock (page 230) or water

BLANQUETTE DE VEAU

This hearty veal stew is a good example of French bourgeois cooking at its best. We suggest serving it over Rice Pilaf *(page 192)*, potatoes, or buttered noodles.

SERVES 6

In a stockpot or Dutch oven, combine the Chicken Stock, veal, onion, celery, leeks, garlic, 3 ounces of the mushrooms (approximately 6 mushrooms), thyme, parsley, and 1½ teaspoons of the salt. Bring to a boil and then set to a simmer for 2 hours, skimming frequently.

Meanwhile, bring a medium saucepan of water to a boil. Blanch the pearl onions for 5 minutes, drain, and set aside.

In a medium sauté pan, heat the olive oil over a high flame. Add the remaining mushrooms and ¼ teaspoon of salt, and sauté for 5 minutes, until soft and browned. Add the reserved pearl onions and set aside.

When the veal is finished simmering, strain through a colander, catching the stock in a bowl. There should be 3 cups of stock remaining; if there's more, reduce in a medium saucepan over a high flame,

and if there's less, add water or Chicken Stock to make up the difference. Separate the veal from the vegetables, set the veal aside, and discard the vegetables. Keep the remaining stock warm on the stove.

Now make the *velouté*, or white sauce: In the same pot used to cook the veal, melt the butter over a low flame. Add the flour and mix with a wooden spoon until a pale smooth paste forms, about 1 minute. Whisk in the reserved warm stock, 1 cup at a time, making sure that each cup is fully incorporated before adding the next. When all the stock has been added, bring to a boil, and then reduce to a simmer for 5 minutes to thicken. Whisk in the heavy cream, crème fraîche, and white pepper. Add the reserved veal, pearl onions, and mushrooms, and stir gently. Simmer for 5 minutes, add the chopped parsley, and serve.

CLEANING LEEKS

Leeks must always be washed well due to the great amount of sand between the leaves. After removing the tough outer leaves, split the leek lengthwise, starting from the root end. Slice as directed in the recipe and submerge the slices in 2 changes of water. Strain and press between kitchen towels to dry.

INGREDIENTS

10 cups Chicken Stock *(page 230)*

3 pounds veal shoulder, cut into 2-inch cubes

1 medium yellow onion, peeled and cut into 8 pieces

1 celery stalk, cut into 1-inch pieces

2 leeks, white parts only, well cleaned *(see Note)* and cut into 1-inch rings

4 garlic cloves, peeled and thinly sliced

1 pound white button mushrooms, cleaned, stemmed, and quartered

5 sprigs of thyme

5 sprigs of flat-leaf parsley

1¾ teaspoons salt

1 pint pearl onions, peeled

3 tablespoons olive oil

3 tablespoons unsalted butter

4 tablespoons all-purpose flour

¾ cup heavy cream

3 tablespoons crème fraîche

¼ teaspoon freshly ground white pepper

2 tablespoons chopped flat-leaf parsley

PORK MILANESE

Here pork chops get the same treatment as the famous Italian veal dish. They are pounded thin, breaded, fried, and then served with a light salad.

SERVES 6

Brush each onion slice with olive oil, sprinkle with a little salt and pepper, and grill or broil using high heat for 4 minutes per side, until nicely charred. Cool to room temperature.

Prepare a tossed salad by combining the mesclun, tomatoes, and grilled onions in a medium bowl. Do not dress the salad until just before serving.

Position a pork chop between 2 pieces of parchment paper and use a mallet to pound each to a ½-inch thickness, especially around the bone. Set aside and repeat with the remaining chops. Set out 3 shallow bowls: one containing the flour; one containing the milk and eggs, lightly beaten; and one containing the panko. Dredge the chops in the flour, tapping off

the excess; dip in the milk–egg mixture; and then coat with the panko. Sprinkle each with a pinch of salt and pepper.

Heat a dry 12-inch sauté pan over a medium flame for about 1 minute, then add 3 tablespoons of the clarified butter or olive oil (or enough to coat the bottom of the pan). When the butter is hot, add 2 breaded pork chops. Brown each side well, about 4 minutes, and be ready to add more clarified butter to the pan if it appears dry. Plate the chops as they finish and continue cooking the rest.

Whisk the vinaigrette and dress the mesclun salad. Place a small heap of salad on top of each chop, and serve with lemon wedges to be squeezed over.

INGREDIENTS

2 medium red onions, sliced ½ inch thick

¼ cup olive oil

Salt

Freshly ground black pepper

½ pound mesclun salad greens

3 large tomatoes, cored and cut into ½-inch dice

6 pork loin chops

1 cup all-purpose flour

½ cup whole milk

4 large eggs

1 cup panko (Japanese bread crumbs)

8 tablespoons (1 stick) butter, clarified *(see page 213)*, or olive oil

¼ cup Balsamic Vinaigrette *(page 237)*

2 lemons, cut into wedges, for serving

BREAD CRUMBS

For this dish, we use Japanese bread crumbs, or panko, because of their thin, jagged shape, which creates a lighter and crisper coating. They can be found at Asian or specialty markets.

PORK TENDERLOIN

WITH SAUTÉED POLENTA

These lean and tender pork medallions are quickly sautéed and then served with rich polenta cakes. The sauce was originally devised at the raw bar for a ceviche, but we discovered it is even more delicious with pork and grilled steaks.

SERVES 6

Heat ¼ cup of the olive oil in a large sauté pan over a medium flame. Add the onions, garlic, and 1 teaspoon of the salt and cook for 5 minutes, stirring occasionally, until the onions are soft and translucent but not brown. Add the red and yellow bell peppers and continue to sauté for 8 to 10 minutes. Remove the pan from the heat and add the remaining cup of olive oil, the vinegar, the juice of 2 of the limes, the ginger, red pepper flakes, cumin, and Worcestershire. Set aside for at least 30 minutes or overnight.

Prepare the polenta according to instructions and keep warm in a 200°F. oven.

Season the pork with the remaining ½ teaspoon of salt and a few grindings of white pepper. Heat a large sauté pan over a high flame for 2 to 3 minutes, then add 2 tablespoons of the vegetable oil. When the oil is very hot and smoking, add half of the pork cutlets, being sure not to crowd the pan. Brown each side for 3 minutes (a piece slightly thicker than ½ inch will take about 4 minutes); the cutlets should be nicely browned on each side. Remove from the pan and repeat with the remaining cutlets.

To serve, bring the sauce to a simmer and add the arugula, basil, tarragon, and oregano. Arrange 2 slices of sautéed polenta on each plate and top with 2 pork cutlets. Spoon the sauce over the pork and finish with a squeeze of the remaining lime.

INGREDIENTS

1¼ cups olive oil

2 medium red onions, diced medium

4 garlic cloves, minced

1½ teaspoons salt

2 red bell peppers, diced medium

2 yellow bell peppers, diced medium

4 tablespoons white-wine vinegar

3 limes

1 teaspoon freshly grated peeled ginger

½ teaspoon red pepper flakes

½ teaspoon cumin

1 teaspoon Worcestershire sauce

Sautéed Mascarpone-Parmesan Polenta *(page 185)*

12 pork tenderloin medallions, ½ inch thick (about 2½ pounds)

Freshly ground white pepper

4 tablespoons vegetable oil

1 cup arugula, cut into slim ribbons

2 tablespoons chopped fresh basil

2 tablespoons chopped fresh tarragon

2 tablespoons chopped fresh oregano

PRUNE-STUFFED
ROAST LOIN OF PORK

This natural pairing of pork and fruit uses one of the most tender cuts of pork, and, if you can find them (try www.zingermans.com), the prunes of Agen are thought to be the best. This is delicious with Potato Gratin *(page 172)*.

SERVES 6

Preheat the oven to 450°F.

Wrap the handle of a wooden spoon in cling wrap, and use it to bore a hole through the length of pork loin, in the center of the meatiest part. If necessary, start things off with the tip of a boning knife. The hole should be not much wider than a thumb and should run from end to end of the roast. Press the prunes into the tunnel, using the wooden spoon handle to push them toward the middle. Work from both sides until the prunes have been threaded throughout. Season with ½ teaspoon of the salt and several grindings of pepper.

Heat a roasting pan over a high flame for about 2 minutes and then add the olive oil. When the oil starts to smoke, add the roast and brown evenly on all sides, al-lowing 3 to 4 minutes before turning, for a deep brown crust. Add the diced carrots, onion, celery, garlic, meat scraps, rose-mary, and sage. Transfer to the oven. Roast for 40 minutes, or until an instant-read thermometer reads 150°F. for a moist roast with a touch of rosy color. Let rest for at least 15 minutes.

Meanwhile, set the roasting pan back on top of the stove over medium heat. Add the white wine, bring to a boil, and use a wooden spoon to stir and scrape the baked-on bits on the bottom of the pan. When the wine has reduced by half, about 3 minutes, add the stock and again reduce by a third. Swirl in the butter, strain out the solids, and keep the jus warm while carving. Serve the roast with the jus passed alongside.

INGREDIENTS

1 boneless center-cut pork
  loin roast, about 4 pounds,
  tied by your butcher

½ cup dried prunes

½ teaspoon salt

  Coarsely ground black
  pepper

⅓ cup olive oil

2 carrots, cut into medium
  dice

1 large yellow onion, cut into
  medium dice

2 celery stalks, cut into
  medium dice

1 head of garlic, halved
  horizontally

1 pound pork scraps
  (including the trimmings
  from the roast)

1 branch of rosemary

3 sprigs of sage

½ cup white wine

1 cup Veal Stock *(page 231)*
  or Chicken Stock *(page 230)*

2 tablespoons unsalted butter

GLAZED PORK BELLY

A fresh slab of bacon, cured, spiced, and braised, isn't for everyone. But for those who love it, this is a magnificent dish. The bacon needs to be cured overnight, so plan ahead. Serve with Pan-Roasted Root Vegetables (*page 198*) or Lentils (*page 193*).

SERVES 6

To cure the pork belly, begin by toasting the spices: Put the cinnamon sticks, star anise, coriander seeds, fennel seeds, and peppercorns into a dry skillet. Place over a medium flame for about 5 minutes, shaking the pan almost constantly, until the aromas of the spices fill the air. Wrap the toasted spices in cheesecloth or a kitchen towel and smash them with a mallet or other heavy kitchen tool.

In a large bowl, combine half of the toasted spices with the salt, sugar, bay leaves, thyme, sage, rosemary, and garlic. Rub the spices all over the pork and bury it in the bowl. Cover with plastic wrap and refrigerate for 24 hours. Take the remaining half of the toasted spices, wrap with cheesecloth, and tie with butcher's twine, creating a spice sachet.

The next day, remove the pork and rinse away the salt cure. Cut the slab of pork (slice along the grain, not across it) into 2 pieces for ease of handling. Gather up the herbs and the crushed garlic cloves and discard the salt.

Preheat the oven to 350°F.

Heat the olive oil in a heavy-bottomed 10×14-inch roasting pan (large enough

to comfortably hold the slabs of pork, leaving at least a 1-inch border all around). Trim the pieces of pork if need be. When the oil smokes, add the onion and sauté for 8 to 10 minutes, until it begins to caramelize. Add the celery and carrots and cook for 5 minutes, stirring frequently. Add the pineapple and continue to cook for 5 minutes more. When the contents of the pot looks brown and savory, add the tomato paste and stir for about 2 minutes. Then add the fresh tomatoes, the spice sachet, and the herbs and garlic rescued from the salt cure. Stir well to combine. Add the white wine, raise the flame to high, and reduce to a few tablespoons, about 3 minutes.

Place the pork belly, rind side up, in the pan and pour in enough stock to fill the pan but not cover the meat. The liquid should be just level with the top layer of fat. Still over a high flame, bring it to a simmer. Transfer the uncovered pot to the oven and cook for 2 hours, basting every 15 minutes to create a burnished glaze on the fatty rind of the meat. Add Veal Stock as needed to keep the pan filled and simmering. The liquid should stay at the same level throughout the cooking process. When all the Veal Stock has been used, add water (about 1 quart).

Remove the pork to a plate and strain the sauce into a medium saucepan. Bring to a simmer and skim away any of the fat that

appears on the surface. Reduce the liquid by half, about 15 minutes, at which point it should be a rich glaze. Adjust the seasoning if necessary. Slice the pork across its width, into thick slices, and serve with the rich sauce spooned over.

INGREDIENTS

2 cinnamon sticks
6 whole star anise
1 tablespoon coriander seeds
1 tablespoon fennel seeds
1 tablespoon black peppercorns
3 cups kosher salt
1 cup sugar
2 bay leaves
4 sprigs of thyme
2 sprigs of sage
1 sprig of rosemary
6 garlic cloves, peeled and crushed
1 slab of fresh pork belly, about 5 pounds

¼ cup olive oil
1 large onion, cut into ½-inch dice
2 celery stalks, cut into ½-inch dice
3 medium carrots, cut into ½-inch dice
1 cup diced fresh pineapple
2 tablespoons tomato paste
3 plum tomatoes, peeled, seeded, and diced *(see page 244)*
1 cup dry white wine
1 quart Veal Stock *(page 231)*

STUFFED SADDLE OF LAMB

The saddle—located exactly where you'd expect it to be—is comprised of three desirable cuts: the buttery-soft tenderloin, the loin, and the flank, constructed in such a way that stuffing and rolling the whole thing seems practically intuitive. The outer layer of fat lards the otherwise lean meat, making the roast self-basting. In the center of this dish, greens, mushrooms, and herbs add their usual color, flavor, and aroma. This is an impressive all-season presentation that's pretty simple to make.

SERVES 4

INGREDIENTS

7 tablespoons olive oil

1½ cups Swiss chard, cleaned

1½ cups arugula, cleaned

1 cup spinach, cleaned

1 medium yellow onion, cut into ½-inch dice (about 1 cup)

1 cup white mushrooms, diced small

1 cup shiitake mushrooms, stemmed and diced small

½ cup chopped fresh basil
  Salt
  Freshly ground white pepper

½ saddle of lamb, boneless (6 or 7 pounds), with flank pounded to a ½-inch thickness (you can have the butcher take care of this)

2 tablespoons vegetable oil

2 garlic cloves

1 sprig of rosemary

Preheat the oven to 400°F.

Heat 2 tablespoons of the olive oil in a large sauté pan over a medium flame. Add the Swiss chard, arugula, and spinach and gently toss until the leaves are wilted but still have some crunch to them, about 2 minutes. Transfer to a colander to cool.

Add 2 more tablespoons of olive oil to the pan over medium-low heat. Add the onion and cook, stirring frequently, for 10 minutes, until soft but not brown. Pour the cooked onion into the colander with the greens. Add the remaining 3 tablespoons of olive oil to the pan and increase the heat to medium-high. Add the white mushrooms and shiitakes and sauté until nicely browned, about 10 minutes. Add the mushrooms to the colander and press the contents to squeeze out excess moisture and fat. Add the basil, a pinch of salt, and a pinch of white pepper, and toss to combine.

Working on a large cutting board or baking sheet, season the lamb loin, tenderloin, and flank with ¼ teaspoon of the salt and ¼ teaspoon of the white pepper. Cut 6 pieces of butchers twine, about 12 inches each, and lay them on the board, left to right, about 2 inches apart. Place the saddle of lamb, skin side down, loin nearest to you (that's the thick side) and flank (thinner side) farthest away and perpendicular to the lengths of twine. Hold the tenderloin aside. Spread the greens-mushroom mixture evenly across the flank, leaving a 2-inch border along the edges of the meat. Tuck the tenderloin across the top of the loin and roll it up tightly inside with the flank. Bind the meat with the lengths of twine (it's easiest to tie the middle first, then each end).

Heat a large ovenproof sauté pan or roasting pan over a high flame. Add the vegetable oil. When it begins to smoke, add the rolled lamb and brown well on all sides, about 3 minutes per side. Add the garlic and rosemary to the pan and place in the preheated oven. For medium, cook for 25 minutes (or until the internal temperature is 140°F.); for well-done, about 30 minutes (or an internal temperature of 160°F.). Bear in mind that the cooking process continues outside of the oven so remove the meat when its temperature is 10 degrees less than the desired outcome. Let the roast rest for 10 minutes before cutting into 1-inch slices to serve.

SADDLE OF LAMB

This is a pricey piece of meat that requires an advance order with your butcher. The cut serves 4 abundantly or 6 barely (there wouldn't be any left for the all-important second helpings). As it isn't much more work to roast 2 saddles side by side, consider doubling the recipe for dinners of 6 to 8 people. And if stuffing and tying such a large roast is intimidating, it's perfectly acceptable to bring your homemade stuffing to the butcher and ask him to do it.

BRAISED LAMB SHOULDER

The shoulder is an imposing piece of meat. Try putting this large hunk in a stew pot whole and the reward will be long buttery-soft hunks with remarkable texture. Serve with Socca (*page 182*) and a salad of lightly dressed arugula. Place an advance order with your butcher for this cut of meat.

SERVES 6

Season both sides of the two lamb pieces with the salt and pepper. Heat the vegetable oil in a large Dutch oven over a medium-high flame and when it begins to smoke, brown each piece of lamb, about 3 minutes per side. Set aside.

Reduce the heat to medium and add the chopped onion, fennel, carrot, celery, and the garlic. Cook until the vegetables are soft and slightly brown, about 5 minutes. Add the tomato paste and the 2 chopped tomatoes, stir, and cook for 2 minutes. Add the flour, stir well to combine, and then add the wine. Raise the flame to high and reduce the liquid by half, about 7 to 10 minutes. Return the browned lamb to the pot and add the stock, rosemary, and thyme. Bring to a simmer, cover with a tight-fitting lid, and cook for 3 hours. Check the lamb every now and then to skim any foam that might accumulate.

After 3 hours, the lamb should be incredibly tender. Remove the meat from the pot and set aside. Strain the sauce through a colander, return the liquid to the pot, and discard the solids. Bring the sauce to a boil and reduce by half, using a large metal spoon to skim the oily fat that accumulates on the surface.

Meanwhile, pull the meat from the bones in finger-size pieces, discarding any veins of fat that you encounter. When you have 4 cups of sauce bubbling away in the pot, add the lamb pieces, the bell peppers, the 3 diced tomatoes, and the basil. Stir to blend, and simmer for 5 minutes.

Serve in deep bowls, with rolled Socca alongside.

INGREDIENTS

1 shoulder of lamb, 7 to
9 pounds, blade separated
and all excess fat trimmed

2 teaspoons salt

2 teaspoons coarsely ground
black pepper

3 tablespoons vegetable oil

1 onion, roughly chopped

½ fennel bulb, roughly
chopped

1 large carrot, roughly
chopped

2 celery stalks, including
leafy tops, roughly chopped

½ head of garlic, cut
horizontally

2 tablespoons tomato paste

5 large tomatoes, 2 roughly
chopped and 3 diced

3 tablespoons all-purpose
flour

2 cups white wine

8 cups Veal Stock *(page 231)*

3 sprigs of rosemary

6 sprigs of thyme

2 roasted yellow bell peppers,
peeled and cut into ¼-inch
strips *(see page 249)*

2 roasted red bell peppers,
peeled and cut into ¼-inch
strips *(see page 249)*

¼ cup basil leaves, cut into
⅛-inch ribbons

CHAMPVALLON

This dish won the favor of King Louis XIV, who apparently had a thing for women who were talented in the kitchen. He secretly married its inventor and packed off her predecessor, who had earlier seduced him with her own mutton chops en papillote. We too have enjoyed enormous success with this homey layering of lamb, potatoes, and onions.

SERVES 6

Season the lamb with ½ teaspoon of the salt and the pepper. Heat 2 tablespoons of the oil in a large sauté pan over a medium-high flame. When the oil is smoking, begin browning the meat in three batches. In order to form a nice crust, let the pan get very hot and let the meat sizzle, undisturbed, for about 3 minutes per side. After each batch is finished, remove the meat to a bowl, spill out the fat, replace the pan over a high flame, and pour in about ¼ cup of the stock, which will bubble up immediately. Use a wooden spoon to scrape the bottom of the pan and free up the browned bits that adhere to it. When the pan has been scraped clean and the stock has taken on a deep brown color, remove the pan from the heat and spill its contents into the bowl with the browned lamb. Wipe the pan relatively clean with a paper towel, replenish with another 2 tablespoons of oil, and brown the next group. After the third deglazing is complete, rather than spill the broth out into the bowl with the lamb, add the onions, garlic, thyme, bay leaf, and the remaining ½ teaspoon of salt. Cook for 10 minutes, stirring occasionally. Add the browned lamb to the pot, along with the remaining stock. Bring to a boil, reduce to a gentle simmer, and cook for 1 hour.

Preheat the oven to 400°F.

When the lamb has finished simmering, peel and slice the potatoes very thin, preferably using a mandoline. Rinse the potatoes in cold water to remove some of the starch. Cover the bottom of a 12-inch, straight-sided ovenproof sauté pan with half the potatoes. Form concentric circles, starting at the outer edge, overlapping each slice by half. Spoon all of the lamb and its cooking broth over that, and top with the rest of the potatoes arranged in the same fashion. Use your hand to press the top layer down, fully moistening the potatoes with the broth. Bake for 1 hour basting the potatoes every 20 minutes. (Slant the pan toward you and a pool of broth will form from which you can spoon out some liquid.) Serve hot from the oven.

INGREDIENTS

2 pounds boneless lamb
  shoulder, cut into small
  cubes

1 teaspoon salt

½ teaspoon freshly ground
  black pepper

6 tablespoons olive oil

3½ cups Chicken Stock
  (page 230)

1½ large onions, peeled,
  halved, and thinly sliced

2 garlic cloves, peeled and
  thinly sliced

1 teaspoon chopped fresh
  thyme

1 bay leaf

2 Idaho potatoes

CHAMPVALLON

A fatty cut works best here; the short braising period will turn leaner cuts tough. The lamb, which is browned in batches, leaves some of its important flavor in the pan. As a method of capturing these browned bits of flavor before they burn and turn bitter, deglaze the pan between batches with a little of the Chicken Stock. It's a tiny extra step but the results are superior. And besides, it also allows you to brown the meat on full throttle with no fear of a bitter broth.

ROAST LEG OF LAMB

WITH ROSEMARY AND VEGETABLES

Simple and satisfying, a roast leg of lamb is one dish that everyone should know how to make. It can feed six easily or four with some left over for sandwiches. A lamb sandwich with homemade Mayonnaise *(page 250)* is reason enough to make leg of lamb a weekly Sunday dinner.

SERVES 4 TO 6

PHOTOGRAPH BY CHRISTOPHER HIRSHEIMER

Preheat the oven to 450°F.

Set an empty roasting pan over 2 burners and heat the pan over a high flame. Add the vegetable oil. Rub salt over the lamb and then follow with the generous amount of pepper. When the oil is smoking hot, add the leg of lamb (carefully, so as not to spatter hot oil), rounder side first. Use tongs and a spatula to turn the leg after about 5 minutes, or when a dark brown crust has formed. After another 5 minutes, turn off both burners, add the rosemary and garlic to the pan, and transfer to the oven.

After the lamb has been in the oven for 15 minutes, add the potatoes and carrots to the pan, tossing them to coat with oil. Continue to cook, stirring the vegetables every 10 minutes, for 30 minutes more.

For lamb with a pink center (medium-rare), an instant-read thermometer should register 135°F. Cook until the thermometer reads 140°F. for medium. Let the lamb rest on a platter for 10 minutes before carving. Use a slotted spoon to transfer the vegetables to a serving bowl.

To make a quick gravy, spoon out all but 1 tablespoon of fat from the pan. Set the pan back on the stovetop and turn the heat to medium-high. Add the stock (or water), along with any meat juices that have collected on the cooling platter of lamb, and bring to a boil. Use a wooden spoon to scrape up any drippings from the bottom of the pan. Reduce the liquid by half, about 10 minutes, and then stir in the butter to finish. Strain.

Cut thick slices of lamb, and serve with the roasted vegetables and gravy.

INGREDIENTS

¼ cup vegetable oil

2 tablespoons coarse salt

2 teaspoons coarsely ground black pepper

1 leg of lamb, about 6 pounds, on the bone, trimmed but not stripped of all fat

3 sprigs of rosemary

1 head of garlic, halved horizontally

6 medium Yukon gold potatoes, cut into 8 pieces

1 pound baby carrots, washed and trimmed

2 cups Chicken Stock *(page 230)*

2 tablespoons unsalted butter

CHOUCROUTE GARNIE

Brasseries began as simple beer halls in Alsace. In the mid–nineteenth century, rather grand-looking railway stations began to spring up, and the design of their dining rooms took on a similar opulence. Despite these lavish interiors, brasseries still managed to retain the diverse clientele and boisterous atmosphere of the original beer halls. Choucroute Garnie, standard fare since its Alsatian beginnings, remains a testimony to a simple and hearty style of eating.

Although the word *choucroute* means sauerkraut, or "bitter herb," the braised cabbage supports the dish's many and varied meats, including veal and pork sausages, smoked bacon, ham hocks, and pork loins. (If you can't find any of the individual meats, make up for their absence by increasing the amount of whatever you do find. On-line sausage buying can be done at schallerweber.com.) Serve with small dishes of whole-grain mustard and boiled potatoes.

SERVES 6

INGREDIENTS

3 pounds sauerkraut
½ pound smoked slab bacon
8 whole cloves
½ cup duck fat, bacon grease, or lard
1 teaspoon ground cumin seed
1 teaspoon juniper berries
1 tablespoon black peppercorns
2 bay leaves
1 pound yellow onions, sliced (2½ large onions)
1 teaspoon salt
2 garlic cloves, peeled and finely minced

1 smoked ham hock
1 pound kassler ripchen (smoked pork loin)
1 herb sachet (2 branches of rosemary, 4 branches of thyme, 2 bay leaves, 2 branches of sage, and 6 branches of flat-leaf parsley)
1 bottle Riesling
3 bratwurst
3 knockwurst
3 beef frankfurters
3 weiswurst (bockwurst)

The day before you plan to cook, put the sauerkraut in a large bowl and cover with cold water. Soak for 24 hours. The next day, strain it into a large colander, rinse under cold water, and press to remove as much liquid as possible.

Preheat the oven to 350°F.

Stud the slab of bacon with the cloves.

Melt the duck fat over medium heat in a very large Dutch oven or stock-pot. When it has melted completely, add the cumin, juniper, peppercorns, and bay leaves. Stir for 1 to 2 minutes to toast the spices and infuse the fat with their flavor. Add the onions and salt and cook for about 12 to 15 minutes, until the onions are soft and just beginning to take on color. Add the drained sauerkraut along with the chopped garlic, mix well, and cook for 10 minutes.

Add the slab of bacon, the hock, the pork loin, and the herb sachet, and stir well to combine. Pour in the Riesling, cover with a tight-fitting lid, transfer to the oven, and cook for 90 minutes.

Add the 4 types of sausages. Gauge the moisture in the pot: It should be wet but not soupy. If need be, add about 1 cup chicken stock, Riesling, or water, just enough to moisten. Cook the sausages, covered, for 10 minutes.

To serve, use tongs to transfer the sauerkraut to a large serving platter or bowl. (Cast-iron enameled cookware can go right to the table, but be sure to remove the herb sachet and bay leaves.) Slice the pork loin and the slab bacon. Cut all the sausages in half and then arrange all of the meat over the sauerkraut.

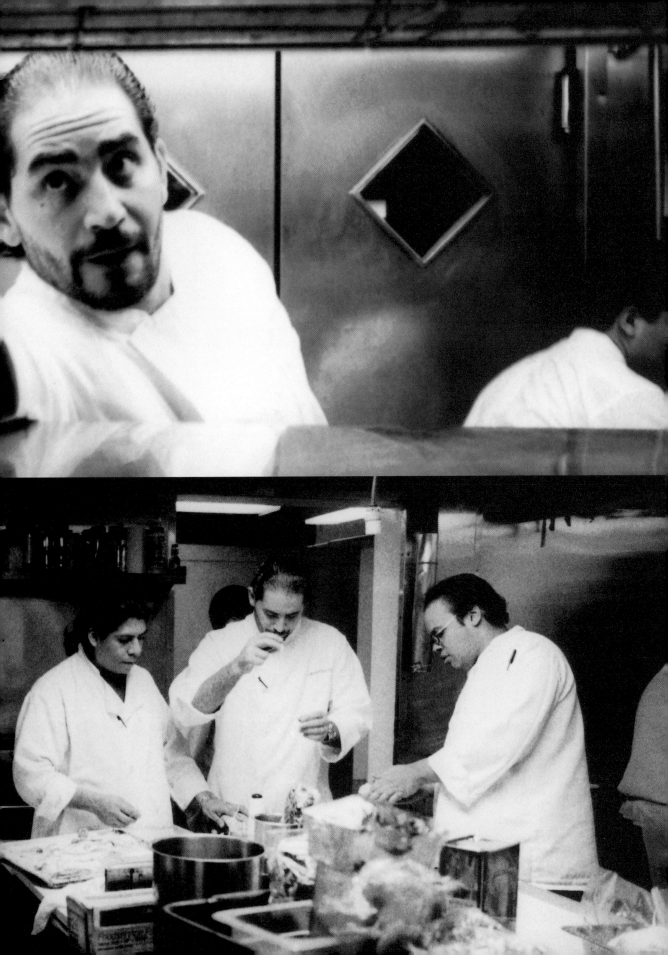

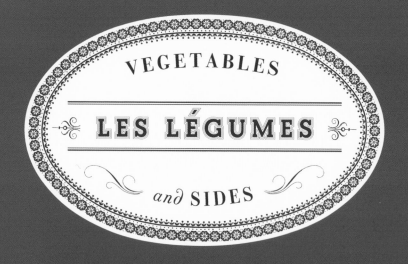

VEGETABLES

LES LÉGUMES

and SIDES

FRENCH FRIES

I n building Balthazar, as much time and effort went into the details—the tiny brass studs on the seats of the chairs, the narrow strips of zinc holding up the ancient mirrors—as on the grander aspects of the decor. We felt the same way about the French Fries. They're often taken for granted, or seen as incidental, so for us it became imperative that they be something special. Something that represented Balthazar as much as the more glamorous dishes.

We serve the well-studied double-blanched *frites* invented by the Belgians. They're hand-cut, fried to shades of blond and brown, delivered to the table in paper cones, and served with ketchup and Mayonnaise *(page 250)*; many customers formulate their own special sauce by giving their fries a quick dip in both.

SERVES 6

Peel the potatoes and cut each one lengthwise into ¼-inch-thick slices. Stack a few slices and cut lengthwise every ¼ inch, resulting in fries that are about 4 to 5 inches long and ¼-inch thick.

Transfer the sliced potatoes to a large bowl and cover with water. Refrigerate and soak for at least 12 hours or overnight. Drain the fries at least 20 minutes before cooking them and dry on kitchen towels.

Pour the peanut oil into a Dutch oven or large saucepan. Attach a candy thermometer to the pot to gauge the oil's temperature and turn on a medium flame. When the oil reaches a temperature of

370°F., add a third of the cut potatoes. The oil temperature will drop to about 280°F. when the potatoes are thrown in. Cook for 3 minutes, remove with a slotted spoon, and set aside on a baking sheet. Return the oil to a temperature of 370°F. and add the next batch. Repeat the process until all the fries are done.

For the second fry, heat the same oil to 380°F. Add half the fries and cook for 3½ minutes, or until golden brown. Remove from the oil and drain on absorbent paper while the other half are frying. Sprinkle with sea salt on a baking sheet and serve as soon as possible.

INGREDIENTS

6 Idaho potatoes	Good-quality sea salt
2 quarts peanut oil	

FRYING FRIES

Idaho potatoes are soaked overnight in water to remove excess starch. The first fry, done at a lower temperature, cooks the potatoes thoroughly, leaving the interior fluffy and tasting only of potato. The second fry, at a higher temperature, crisps the exterior: The sugars of the potato caramelize in the high heat and turn the fries crisp and brown at the edges.

POTATO GRATIN

Creamy, garlicky, and always completely devoured.

Preheat the oven to 375°F.

Combine the heavy cream, milk, garlic, rosemary, thyme, 1 teaspoon of the salt, and ¼ teaspoon of the pepper in a medium saucepan. Bring to a low simmer and cook for 30 minutes. Strain, discard the herbs and garlic, and reserve the flavored cream.

Meanwhile, peel the potatoes and cut them into ⅛-inch slices. Rinse the slices in a large bowl of cold water, then dry on paper towels.

Butter a 10×14-inch gratin dish (you could also use a straight-sided ovenproof sauté pan), using 1 tablespoon of the butter. Arrange a first layer of potatoes in the buttered pan, in rows, overlapping the potatoes by nearly half. Sprinkle the layer with ¼ teaspoon of the salt and a few grindings of white pepper, and pour ½ cup of the garlic-infused cream over. Arrange a second layer of potatoes, repeat the seasoning, and pour another ½ cup of cream over. Repeat with remaining potatoes and cream, about 4 layers. Dot the top with the remaining tablespoon of butter, and cover with aluminum foil.

Bake for 45 minutes, remove the foil, and continue to bake for another 15 minutes, until the top turns golden brown. Cool for 5 minutes before serving.

INGREDIENTS

2 cups heavy cream
1 cup whole milk
7 garlic cloves, crushed with the side of a knife
2 sprigs of rosemary
4 sprigs of thyme

2 teaspoons salt
Freshly ground white pepper
6 Idaho potatoes
2 tablespoons unsalted butter

GARLIC MASHED POTATOES

A ricer or food mill is a worthwhile tool for anyone who loves mashed potatoes. The cells of the potato remain intact while being pressed through the small holes of a ricer instead of breaking as they would with a masher.

SERVES 6

Combine the garlic and cream in a small saucepan over a medium flame. Bring to a boil, turn down to a simmer, and cook for 15 to 30 minutes, until the garlic is very soft. Pour the mixture into a blender and purée. (Keep a firm grip on the lid, as the heat from the cream mixture will force it up.) Set aside, to be reheated later in either a saucepan or in a microwave before adding it to the final dish. (The garlic-infused cream can be prepared a day in advance and stored, covered, in the refrigerator.)

Put the potatoes in a large pot, cover with water by 2 inches, and add 1 tablespoon of the salt. Bring to a boil and cook for 20 to 25 minutes, until the potatoes are tender. Drain in a colander. While still warm, press the potatoes through a ricer into a large bowl. Reheat the garlic-infused cream.

Use a rubber spatula to slowly fold in the butter and the warm garlic cream. Season with the remaining 1 tablespoon of salt and the pepper. Serve immediately.

INGREDIENTS

10 garlic cloves, peeled and cut in thirds

2 cups heavy cream

6 Idaho potatoes, peeled and cut into 2-inch cubes

2 tablespoons salt

¾ pound (3 sticks) unsalted butter, at room temperature, cut into cubes

1 teaspoon freshly ground white pepper

CRUSHED POTATOES

S erve this as a warm side dish, or add Sweet-and-Sour Shallots *(page 242)* and serve at room temperature as a potato salad.

SERVES 6

Preheat the oven to 450°F.

Wrap each potato in aluminum foil and bake for 45 minutes, or until tender on the fork. Remove from the oven and let cool from hot to warm.

Discard the foil and remove the skins with a paring knife. In a large bowl, lightly crush the potatoes with a fork. Mix in the olive oil, salt, and pepper to taste.

INGREDIENTS

8 Yukon gold potatoes	1 tablespoon salt
¼ cup extra-virgin olive oil	Freshly ground white pepper

POTATO GNOCCHI

Eating gnocchi in a restaurant is perhaps worth making a reservation for. Eating gnocchi in someone's home (unless they live with their Italian grandmother or intend to put out) should generally be avoided. But with some practice, success can be achieved at home. Serve with any of the braised dishes.

SERVES 6

Preheat the oven to 400°F.

Wrap the potatoes in aluminum foil and bake for 40 minutes. Be careful not to overbake; the potatoes shouldn't be mushy.

Unwrap the potatoes. As soon as they're cool enough to handle, remove their skins. Run the warm potatoes through a food mill or ricer and allow to cool completely in a large bowl.

Add the egg, Parmesan, 1 teaspoon of the salt, the pepper, and nutmeg to the riced potatoes. Using your hands, mix just enough to incorporate. Add the flour and quickly knead the dough until it comes together as a soft and slightly sticky mass. If the dough is too wet to handle, add a bit more flour and continue to quickly but loosely knead.

Form the dough into a mass and cut into 4 parts. Cover 3 parts with a clean dish towel and begin working with 1. On a large, lightly floured cutting board, roll the dough into a long rope, about $\frac{1}{2}$ to

$\frac{3}{4}$ inch thick. Cut into gnocchis that are about 1 inch long. Repeat with the remaining parts. When all the dough has been rolled and cut, give each one a ridged shape by rolling them over the tines of a fork.

To cook, prepare an ice-water bath in a large bowl and bring a large pot of salted water to a boil. Add the gnocchi to the boiling water and cook for about 5 minutes, or until they rise to the surface. Use a slotted spoon to transfer them to the ice bath. Cool for a minute and then transfer to a paper-towel-lined baking sheet to dry; sprinkle with the remaining $\frac{1}{2}$ teaspoon of salt. Use immediately or cover with plastic wrap and refrigerate overnight.

To sauté, melt the butter in a large sauté pan. Heat until it begins to turn a nut-brown, about 5 minutes. Add the gnocchi, toss to coat with butter, and sauté for 8 to 10 minutes, stirring occasionally, until they take on a buttery-golden appearance.

INGREDIENTS

- 4 medium Idaho potatoes
- 1 whole extra-large egg, beaten
- 1 tablespoon freshly grated Parmesan cheese
- 1½ teaspoons salt
- ¼ teaspoon freshly ground white pepper
- ⅛ teaspoon freshly grated nutmeg
- 1 cup all-purpose flour plus additional if necessary
- 8 tablespoons (1 stick) unsalted butter

POTATOES FOR GNOCCHI

Use starchy Idaho baking potatoes. Cook them in their skins and then churn through a ricer when they're still warm. Over-handling the dough is a no-no; knead just enough to get the job done.

POMMES À LA SARLADAISE

In the Périgord region, where ducks and geese are raised primarily for their livers, the fat is naturally used for frying. The town of Sarlat is best known for the most savory fried potatoes ever. They're an obvious companion to Duck Confit (*page 111*), and, when served with eggs, make for an excellent Sunday breakfast. Missing from this recipe are black truffles, the other prize of the Périgord. If you have the bucks to have one on hand, shave a few slices over the potatoes a few minutes before serving. (Rendered goose or duck fat is available at most specialty markets or through D'Artagnan, www.dartagnan.com.)

SERVES 6

Bring a medium saucepan of salted water to a boil. Add the potatoes and cook for 6 to 8 minutes, until tender yet still holding their shape. Drain and spread the potatoes on a baking sheet to cool to room temperature.

The potatoes will be sautéed in 3 batches. Heat 3 tablespoons of duck fat in a large sauté pan over a high flame. When it begins to smoke, add one third of the potatoes. Shake them into a single layer and let them cook, undisturbed, for about 5 minutes, or until they have developed a deep brown crust. Brown well on all sides and then pour them into a colander to drain. Replace the 3 tablespoons of duck fat in the pan, heat to the smoking point, and repeat the process with the second group of potatoes, and again with the third.

When all the potatoes have been fried and drained, turn the flame to low and melt the butter in the pan. Add the garlic and cook gently for 2 minutes, until it has softened. Add the potatoes, parsley, salt, and pepper, toss gently to combine and reheat, and serve.

INGREDIENTS

6 medium Yukon gold potatoes, peeled and cut into ½-inch dice

½ cup plus 1 tablespoon duck or goose fat

4 tablespoons unsalted butter

1 tablespoon minced garlic (about 1 clove)

2 tablespoons chopped flat-leaf parsley

¼ teaspoon salt

Pinch of white pepper

BUCKWHEAT CREPES

WITH EGGS, HAM, AND GRUYÈRE

On Paris streets, the crepe is a quick snack made by vendors wielding peculiar wooden utensils that spread the batter over hot, round griddles. In a matter of seconds they pour, flip, fill, and fold, then slip the finished product into a parchment packet. Here is a savory crepe to serve at breakfast or lunch. The first crepe you make is always a test flight: Watch how it behaves in the pan in order to gauge the heat and amount of batter needed.

SERVES 6

INGREDIENTS

½ cup buckwheat flour
½ cup all-purpose flour
1 teaspoon salt
14 large eggs
1¾ cups whole milk

8 tablespoons (1 stick)
  unsalted butter,
  4 tablespoons melted
12 thin slices French ham
¾ pound Gruyère, grated

BUCKWHEAT

The hearty buckwheat plant thrives in regions with very unfavorable conditions. It's the foundation of many of the world's peasant diets, including Russia's famous blini, Japan's revered soba noodles, and Brittany's wonderful crepes.

Sift the flours and ½ teaspoon of the salt into a medium bowl. Whisk in 2 of the eggs, 1½ cups of the milk, and then 2 tablespoons of the melted butter. Whisk until smooth. Cover the bowl with plastic wrap and refrigerate for 30 minutes or as long as overnight.

Preheat the oven to 200°F.

Remove the batter from the refrigerator and whisk in the remaining ¼ cup of milk.

Heat an 8-inch nonstick pan over a medium flame. Add ½ teaspoon of the melted butter and use a crumpled paper towel to spread evenly. Hold the pan off the flame and ladle in a scant ¼ cup of batter. Quickly tilt the pan to completely cover the surface with a thin and even circle of batter, return the pan to the heat, and cook the first side for 1 minute, until the edges are brown and the center is dotted with air bubbles. Use your fingers or tongs to turn the crepe onto the other side and cook for 15 seconds more. Stack finished crepes on a plate and keep warm in the oven. Add a new ½ teaspoon of butter to the pan for each crepe.

To scramble the eggs, use a fork or a whisk to blend the remaining 12 eggs, the remaining ½ teaspoon of salt, and 2 tablespoons of water in a large bowl. Over a moderately low flame, melt the remaining 4 tablespoons of butter in a 12-inch nonstick skillet. Pour the eggs in and begin stirring with a wooden spoon. Slowly drag the spoon around the bottom and sides of the pan. After about 5 minutes, the mixture will begin to thicken. Continue stirring until the eggs have formed loosely knit and moist curds, about 8 minutes. Turn off the heat, and set aside.

To finish the crepes, preheat the oven to 400°F.

Lay a crepe, darker side down, on a lightly buttered baking pan. Layer a slice of ham, a sprinkling of Gruyère, and a single portion of the scrambled eggs, about ¼ cup. Roll the crepe and place seam side down on the pan. Repeat with the remaining crepes, and bake for 5 minutes. Serve hot from the oven.

SOCCA

These chickpea pancakes are the street snack of Nice, where they're cooked on giant steel pie sheets in wood-fired ovens. Cooked in local olive oil, they're scraped into paper cones for sidewalk consumption. Besides serving these alongside the Braised Lamb Shoulder *(page 158)*, use them as you would a flatbread or savory crepe. Golden and nutty chickpea flour is available in health food stores.

MAKES 15 PANCAKES

In a medium bowl, sift together the all-purpose flour, chickpea flour, and the salt and pepper. In another bowl, whisk together the cream, egg, and 2½ cups of water. Gently whisk the wet ingredients into the dry until smooth. Cover with plastic wrap and let the batter rest in the fridge for at least 1 hour. Just before making the pancakes, add 2 tablespoons of the olive oil to the batter and give it a quick whisk.

Heat an 8-inch nonstick pan over a medium flame until the pan is quite hot. Add ½ teaspoon of olive oil and let heat for about 30 seconds. Pull the pan from the stove and, working quickly so as not to let things cool down, pour in ¼ cup of batter (use a ¼-cup dry measuring cup as a ladle). Tilt the pan as if making a crepe to distribute the batter thinly and evenly. Cook for about 1 minute on the first side (the edges will be dry) and about 30 seconds on the second side. If the batter is too thick, add a few tablespoons of water to adjust. Repeat with the remaining batter, adding a fresh ½ teaspoon of oil to the pan before each addition of batter. Cool each pancake briefly on a rack before stacking on a plate in a warm oven. The pancakes can be made a day ahead of time, wrapped in plastic, and kept in the refrigerator. Bring to room temperature before warming them in a low oven.

INGREDIENTS

1 cup all-purpose flour
2 cups chickpea flour
1½ teaspoons salt
¼ teaspoon freshly ground white pepper

½ cup heavy cream
1 large egg
3 tablespoons olive oil

MASCARPONE-PARMESAN POLENTA

For some people, polenta will only ever taste as good as what comes with it. But this version, with mascarpone and Parmesan, can stand on its own, as well as complement most meat dishes. The basic technique yields soft polenta, to be served in mounds; frying or grilling it produces firm pieces. Grilled polenta requires chilling, so start well in advance.

SERVES 6

Bring the stock to a boil in a saucepan. Keep warm over a medium flame.

In a medium saucepan, bring the milk and half-and-half to a foamy simmer. Reduce the flame to medium and add the polenta to the foaming milk mixture, stirring continuously. When the mixture begins to thicken, begin adding the hot stock, ½ cup at a time. As with risotto, let the stock absorb completely before adding the next ½ cup, stirring all the while.

When all of the stock has been added, reduce the flame to low and add the butter,

mascarpone, and Parmesan, stirring well to blend. If the consistency overall is too thick, add a bit of milk or stock. Stir in the salt and pepper.

Spoon-serve immediately or grill in the following manner: Spread the soft polenta in a buttered casserole dish or sheet pan and refrigerate for at least 4 hours, or overnight. Cut 3-inch circles from the cooled pan and either pan-fry in 2 tablespoons of oil or grill, lightly brushed with oil.

INGREDIENTS

2 cups Chicken Stock
   (page 230)
2 cups whole milk
2 cups half-and-half
2 cups dry cornmeal polenta
8 tablespoons (1 stick)
   unsalted butter, cut in
   pieces

1 cup mascarpone
½ pound grated Parmesan
   (about 1 cup)
¼ teaspoon salt
⅛ teaspoon freshly ground
   black pepper

MACARONI GRATIN

This delicious gratin is flavored with sharp Gruyère and smoky lardons. It's served at the restaurant in individual casseroles, but it looks best at home in a great big dish. This makes generous portions or highly prized leftovers. Be sure not to overbake the gratin or it will "break," meaning that the butterfat in the cheese will separate from the milk solids, resulting in the dreaded greasy gratin.

SERVES 6 TO 8

Preheat the oven to 400°F.

Cook the macaroni according to the directions on the box. Drain, toss with the olive oil, and set aside in a large mixing bowl.

Add the bacon to a small skillet and sauté over medium heat until brown but not crisp, about 10 minutes. Drain on paper towels and add to the cooked macaroni.

In a medium saucepan, bring the milk just to a foamy boil, then reduce the heat to very low to keep warm. In another saucepan, melt the butter over medium heat. When the foam subsides, remove from the heat. Whisk in the flour and continue stirring until a smooth, pale roux has formed. Return the saucepan to medium heat and, while still whisking steadily, begin ladling the hot milk into the roux, 1 cup at a time, completely incorporating each cup before adding the next. After all the milk has been added, continue to whisk until the sauce thickens and bubbles gently, about 2 minutes. Add the Parmesan, 2 cups of the Gruyère, and the salt and pepper, and stir until the cheese has completely melted.

Pour the sauce over the macaroni, mix thoroughly, and pour into a buttered 10 × 14-inch gratin dish. Bake in the oven for 12 minutes. Remove, sprinkle the remaining cup of Gruyère over the top, and continue baking for an additional 10 minutes, until the top is golden and crunchy.

GRUYÈRE

We use Swiss Gruyère for its distinctively sharp flavor and great ability to melt smoothly and evenly. Good substitutes would be Emmentaler or Comté.

INGREDIENTS

1 16-ounce box of elbow macaroni

2 tablespoons olive oil

4 ounces lightly smoked slab bacon, cut into ¼-inch dice

5 cups whole milk

4 tablespoons (½ stick) unsalted butter

½ cup all-purpose flour

1 cup grated Parmesan cheese

3 cups grated Gruyère cheese

1½ teaspoons salt

½ teaspoon freshly ground white pepper

FETTUCCINE

WITH WILD MUSHROOMS

The sauce has a delicate texture and intense flavor that's best suited to fresh pasta, which is available in sheets or pre-cut at many supermarkets.

SERVES 6

In a medium saucepan, combine half of the white mushrooms with the dried porcinis, dried shiitake, thyme, garlic, and salt. Add 6 cups of water, bring to a simmer, and cook for 40 minutes to create a broth. Strain through a sieve; discard the solids. Strain the liquid through a coffee filter to remove any grit left by the mushrooms. Return the broth to the pot, bring to a boil, and cook until the liquid has reduced to 3 cups, about 5 minutes. Stir in the cream and mascarpone and bring just to a boil. Remove from the heat and set aside, or cover and refrigerate if using a day later.

Slice the fresh wild mushrooms and the remaining white mushrooms $1/8$ inch thick. Heat 3 tablespoons of the olive oil in a large sauté pan over a medium flame. Sauté the mushrooms (in 2 batches if necessary) until well-browned, about 5 minutes. Add the mushrooms to the cream sauce and reheat the sauce over a low flame.

If using fresh pasta dough: Roll out the dough to $1/16$-inch thickness (setting #1 on a hand-cranked machine). Cut the rolled dough into 12-inch sheets and then pass through the machine fitted with the fettuccine attachment. Flour well, and lay the cut noodles on a cookie sheet.

Bring a large pot of salted water to a boil. Add the pasta and cook for about 30 seconds; it will rise to the surface when it's done. (If using dried fettuccine, follow the cooking instructions on the box.)

Strain the pasta and return it to the pot. Add the warm sauce and the grated Parmesan, stir, and let the mixture come to a simmer. Just before serving, add the spinach or arugula and toss to slightly wilt the leaves.

INGREDIENTS

1½ pounds white button
    mushrooms, cleaned

½ ounce dried porcini
    mushrooms

1 ounce dried shiitake
    mushrooms

6 sprigs of thyme

2 garlic cloves, peeled and
    thinly sliced

1 teaspoon salt

⅔ cup heavy cream

¼ cup mascarpone

1 pound fresh wild mushrooms
    (such as cremini or
    shiitakes)

6 tablespoons olive oil

1 pound pasta dough or
    1½ pounds fresh or dried
    fettuccine

½ cup grated Parmesan cheese

4 ounces baby spinach or
    arugula, washed and dried

RISOTTO

WITH SHRIMP AND RED PEPPERS

Although risotto can share a plate with such diverse ingredients as shellfish, mushrooms, or butter and Parmesan, the method for making this creamy dish remains steadfastly the same, regardless of what you might add to it. Choose either Carnaroli or Arborio rice.

SERVES 6

Bring 5 cups of the stock to a low simmer and keep warm on the stove until needed.

Meanwhile, combine the roasted red peppers with the remaining 1 cup of stock in a small saucepan and bring to a simmer. Cook for 10 minutes. Transfer to the bowl of a food processor and blend until smooth; some very small pieces of pepper will remain.

Dry the shrimp with paper towels and season with $\frac{1}{2}$ teaspoon of the salt and a few grindings of white pepper. Heat 2 tablespoons of the olive oil in a large sauté pan over a high flame for 1 minute. Add half the shrimp and cook for about $1\frac{1}{2}$ minutes per side, until they look like cooked shrimp. Remove with tongs to a plate and than sauté the remaining shrimp in the same oil. Set the cooked shrimp aside.

Melt the butter in a large Dutch oven along with the remaining 2 tablespoons of olive oil over a medium-low flame. Add the onion, garlic, and $\frac{1}{2}$ teaspoon of the salt. Cook, stirring frequently, until the onion is soft and translucent, about 2 minutes. Add the rice and stir for 2 minutes, both to coat each grain and to toast gently. Add the wine and stir until it has been absorbed, about 1 minute.

Begin adding the warm chicken stock, about $\frac{1}{2}$ cup at a time. Stir constantly with a wooden spoon and let each addition be absorbed before adding the next. When the last $\frac{1}{2}$ cup of stock has been absorbed, add the sliced scallions. Then, in 3 increments, stir in the reserved red-pepper purée, again letting each addition be absorbed before adding the next. Taste the rice along the way, cooking it only until it's tender, not to where it's mushy.

Stir in the reserved shrimp, the basil, Parmesan, the remaining $\frac{1}{2}$ teaspoon of salt, and white pepper to taste. Serve immediately.

INGREDIENTS

6 cups Chicken Stock
(page 230)

6 roasted red bell peppers *(see page 249)*, cut into
½-inch dice

30 medium shrimp, peeled and deveined

1½ teaspoons salt
Freshly ground white pepper

4 tablespoons olive oil

2 tablespoons unsalted butter

½ yellow onion, minced

1 garlic clove, minced

2 cups Arborio rice

½ cup white wine

3 scallions, cut into ¼-inch rings on a bias

2 tablespoons chopped fresh basil

½ cup grated Parmesan

PARTIAL COOKING OF RISOTTO

Risotto purists insist on the importance of the full cooking process just before serving. While that is ideal, it's not practical for the home cook who wants to spend time with guests, or for many restaurants where 20 minutes of stirring one dish would bring the pumping rhythm of the kitchen to a halt. To partially cook risotto, follow the recipe to the point where the rice is a firm al dente, reserving ⅓ of the Chicken Stock (2 cups). Spread the risotto on a sheet pan and refrigerate, covered with plastic wrap. Just before serving, heat the reserved stock in a saucepan. Place the partially cooked risotto in a pot over medium-low heat and resume adding the stock according to the recipe completion.

RICE PILAF

French food is based on creating layers of flavors, usually starting with onions and butter. Rice doesn't escape this treatment. In the classic French method, the rice is covered with a wax-paper lid cut to fit inside the pot and rest on the rice, allowing for just a bit of gentle evaporation. In the contemporary home kitchen, a pot with a tight-fitting lid will do just fine. Serve with fish or Blanquette de Veau *(page 144)*.

SERVES 6

Preheat the oven to 350°F.

Wash and rinse the rice in cold water. Drain and set aside. In a medium saucepan, bring the stock to a boil, then turn down the heat to the lowest simmer.

In a large ovenproof pot, melt 8 tablespoons of the butter over medium heat until it foams. Add the onion and garlic and cook until the onion is soft and translucent, about 10 minutes; if it begins to take on color, lower the flame. Add the drained rice and cook, stirring, for 2 minutes, making sure that each grain is coated with butter.

Add the bouquet garni and the hot Chicken Stock, cover, and transfer the pot into the oven.

Cook for 25 minutes, remove, and let the pot stand for 15 minutes. Add the remaining 3 tablespoons of butter and use a fork to fluff the rice. Season with salt and pepper to taste.

INGREDIENTS

1½ cups long-grain rice

3 cups Chicken Stock *(page 230)*

8 tablespoons (1 stick) plus 3 tablespoons unsalted butter

1 medium yellow onion, minced (about 1 cup)

2 garlic cloves, peeled and minced

1 bouquet garni *(see page 31)*

Salt and freshly ground black pepper to taste

LENTILS

The volcanic soil of Auvergne, in central France, produces the small green du Puy lentils, the excellence of which has been recognized by the French government in the form of an Appellation d'Origine Contrôlleé—the same type of designation afforded to wines and cheeses.

SERVES 4 TO 6

Rinse the lentils in cold water and place in a medium saucepan. Cover with 4 cups of cold water, bring to a gentle simmer, and cook for 20 minutes.

Meanwhile, place the bacon and thyme in a small saucepan over a medium flame. When some of the fat has rendered from the bacon, about 2 minutes, add the onion, garlic, and salt, and cook for about

5 minutes, until the onion is translucent. Add the butter, carrot, celery, white pepper, and 1 cup of water. Bring to a simmer and cook for 5 minutes.

Drain the lentils and return them to their saucepan. Add the bacon-vegetable mixture and simmer lightly for 7 to 10 minutes, until the lentils are very tender.

INGREDIENTS

1 cup green lentils, preferably du Puy
2 slices of bacon, diced small
4 sprigs of thyme
½ medium onion, diced small
1 garlic clove, minced

1 teaspoon salt
2 tablespoons unsalted butter
1 medium carrot, diced small
1 celery stalk, diced small
¼ teaspoon freshly ground white pepper

SPAETZLE

paetzle are a cross between noodles and dumplings. They are little ribbons of cooked dough that are then sautéed and served with something delicious as a means of soaking up sauce. Below is the method favored by Austrian housewives (and we all know about Austrian housewives), requiring no special equipment and producing a slightly irregular and rustic result.

SERVES 4

Combine the flour, eggs, and milk in a large bowl. Mix with a wooden spoon until well combined. Cover with plastic wrap and refrigerate for at least 1 hour, or overnight.

Bring 2 stockpots of salted water to a boil. (Using 2 pots cuts time at the stove in half.) Fill a large bowl with ice water and keep it near the stove.

Take the batter out of the fridge and stir. It should be the consistency of thick pancake batter; thin with a little milk or thicken with a bit more flour as necessary.

Spread about ⅛ cup of the batter onto a wooden cutting board, near one of the edges. Spread the batter with a long spatula or knife from the edge of the board inward, about ¼ inch thick. Using the side of the spatula or the blade of a knife, begin pushing thin ribbons of batter into the boiling water, where it will form rough-looking dumplings. When they're finished cooking, about 2 minutes, they'll float to the top. Use a slotted spoon or strainer to remove from the boiling water. Slip them into the ice bath, then drain and toss with olive oil to prevent sticking. The spaetzle can be served as is or, as we serve them in the restaurant, sautéed in butter to a brown, crisp finish. Either way, garnish any of the braised dishes with these delicious dumplings. The Spaetzle can be made a day ahead and sautéed right before serving.

INGREDIENTS

2 cups all-purpose flour
7 large eggs

¼ cup whole milk

WHITE BEANS

Properly cooked, white beans should be swollen and plump, and almost creamy in texture. Any bean, dried or fresh, can be cooked in this manner, but the cooking time will vary. Fresh beans need significantly less time on the stove and do not require an overnight soak or pre-cook. Taste them as they cook to gauge them.

SERVES 4 TO 6

Spread the dried beans out on a baking sheet and pick over to discard any off-color beans or small pebbles. Transfer the beans to a bowl, cover with about 2 quarts of water, and soak overnight.

The next day, pour the beans into a colander and strain. Rinse them under cold running water and then transfer to a stockpot. Cover with 1 quart of water and bring to a boil over a high flame. A thick foam will form on the surface of the boiling water. When the foam subsides, drain the beans through a colander and rinse with warm water.

Cut the green leaves from the leek and discard. Split the white stalk down the center nearly to the root end; the leek should now be split but still held together by the very end. Trim the root end smooth and submerge the leek in 3 changes of water to thoroughly wash.

Return the beans to the stockpot and add the leek, stock, carrot, celery, onion halves, bacon, bouquet garni, bay leaf, peppercorns, garlic, and salt. (There are those who are convinced that salting beans during cooking makes for a tougher bean; we haven't had this experience.) Place over medium-high heat and bring to a boil. If any foam rises to the top, skim it away. Turn the flame down to maintain a gentle simmer and cook until the beans are creamy and tender but still retain their shape, about 45 minutes; the only way to cook beans to perfection is to taste them frequently.

Strain the beans through a colander and remove the vegetables, bacon, bouquet garni and peppercorns, garlic, and bay leaf.

INGREDIENTS

1 pound dried white beans
  (navy, cannellini, or Great
  Northerns)

1 leek

1 quart Chicken Stock
  (page 230)

1 large carrot, peeled and cut
  into thirds

1 celery stalk, cut into thirds

1 medium white onion, halved

¼ pound slab bacon

1 bouquet garni *(see
  page 31)*, including
  1 teaspoon black
  peppercorns

1 bay leaf

1 head of garlic, halved
  horizontally

2 tablespoons coarse salt

PAN-ROASTED ROOT VEGETABLES

Pan-roasting intensifies the flavors and brings out the inherent sweetness of root vegetables. Hot and tender, they can be served alongside any roasted meat. They are also delicious at room temperature or as an excellent party or buffet side dish.

SERVES 6

Heat the olive oil in a large skillet over a medium flame. Add the crushed garlic cloves and sauté for 2 minutes, until the cloves just start to take on color. Add the diced vegetables, including the celery leaves, and thyme and cook over high heat, stirring frequently with a spatula, for 5 minutes. Lower the flame to medium and continue to cook, still stirring frequently, for another 10 minutes. Add a splash of water midway through the cooking time to provide some steam. Just before the end of the cooking time, add the butter. The vegetables should be tender and lightly caramelized. Season with the salt and pepper, and stir in the parsley.

INGREDIENTS

¼ cup olive oil

3 garlic cloves, crushed, skins removed

1 celery root, peeled and diced small

3 medium carrots, peeled and diced small

4 parsnips, peeled and diced small

3 celery stalks, peeled, diced small, leaves retained and finely chopped

2 sprigs of thyme

3 tablespoons unsalted butter

½ teaspoon salt

¼ teaspoon freshly ground black pepper

2 tablespoons chopped flat-leaf parsley

SAUTÉED BROCCOLI RABE

WITH OLIVE OIL AND GARLIC

Broccoli rabe isn't broccoli at all but rather a bitter green. It is very common in Italy and recently more available in the United States.

SERVES 6

Bring a large pot of water to a boil. Add the broccoli rabe and cook for 2 to 3 minutes. Drain in a colander and set aside.

In a large skillet, heat the olive oil over a medium flame until it begins to smoke. Add the garlic and sauté for 2 minutes, until it starts to brown. Add the red pepper flakes and thyme and cook, stirring, for about another 2 minutes, making sure the garlic doesn't burn. Add the broccoli rabe and sauté, using tongs to keep the broccoli rabe moving, thoroughly coating the greens with oil. Cook for 6 to 8 minutes, until tender with just a little snap. Season with salt and pepper to taste and toss well.

Serve immediately or allow to cool, then refrigerate. To reheat, sauté in 3 tablespoons of olive oil until hot.

INGREDIENTS

2 bunches of broccoli rabe, about 2 pounds, stemmed and cut into 3-inch pieces

¼ cup olive oil

6 garlic cloves, peeled and thinly sliced

¼ teaspoon red pepper flakes

3 sprigs of thyme

Salt and freshly ground black pepper to taste

FENNEL GRATIN

We serve Fennel Gratin with the Stuffed Saddle of Lamb *(page 155)*, but it's actually perfect alongside any roasted meat. This short and easy recipe can be committed to memory and made without fuss.

SERVES 6

Preheat the oven to 350°F.

Bring a pot of salted water to a boil and blanch the sliced fennel for 5 minutes. Drain, toss with the salt and pepper, and spread in a buttered 6 × 10-inch casserole or gratin dish. Pour in the cream, toss to coat, and then settle the fennel into an even layer. Cover the dish with foil and bake for 30 minutes. Remove the foil, sprinkle the grated Gruyère over the top, and slip under the broiler until the cheese browns to a crisp coating, about 3 minutes.

INGREDIENTS

6 fennel bulbs, outer layer removed, cut into ¼-inch slices

½ teaspoon salt

⅛ teaspoon freshly ground white pepper

½ cup heavy cream

½ cup grated Gruyère cheese

ONION RINGS

A thermometer is mandatory when deep-frying onions. To obtain a steady temperature in the pot, wait between batches for the oil to heat up before adding the next group of onion rings. Save the oil container and funnel the used oil back into it for storage, re-use, or easier disposal.

SERVES 4 TO 6

Sift 1½ cups of the flour, the baking powder, and the salt into a medium bowl. Form a well in the center and pour in the beer and egg. Whisk, beginning in the center and expanding outward, until a smooth batter forms.

Separate the onion slices into rings. Dust the rings with the remaining ½ cup of flour.

In a large, deep pot over a medium-high flame, heat the peanut oil until it registers 360°F. on a candy thermometer. Dredge 5 or 6 of the onion rings in the batter, shake off the excess, and plunge the rings into the hot oil. After 1½ minutes, flip the rings over and cook for another 1½ minutes. Remove the rings with a slotted spoon and drain on a wire rack lined with paper towels. Hold the finished onion rings in a 200°F. oven while the remaining ones are fried. Serve hot.

INGREDIENTS

2 cups all-purpose flour
1 tablespoon plus 1 teaspoon baking powder
1½ teaspoons salt
12 ounces beer (we use Heineken)

1 large egg
1 large Spanish onion, peeled and cut into ½-inch slices
6 cups peanut oil

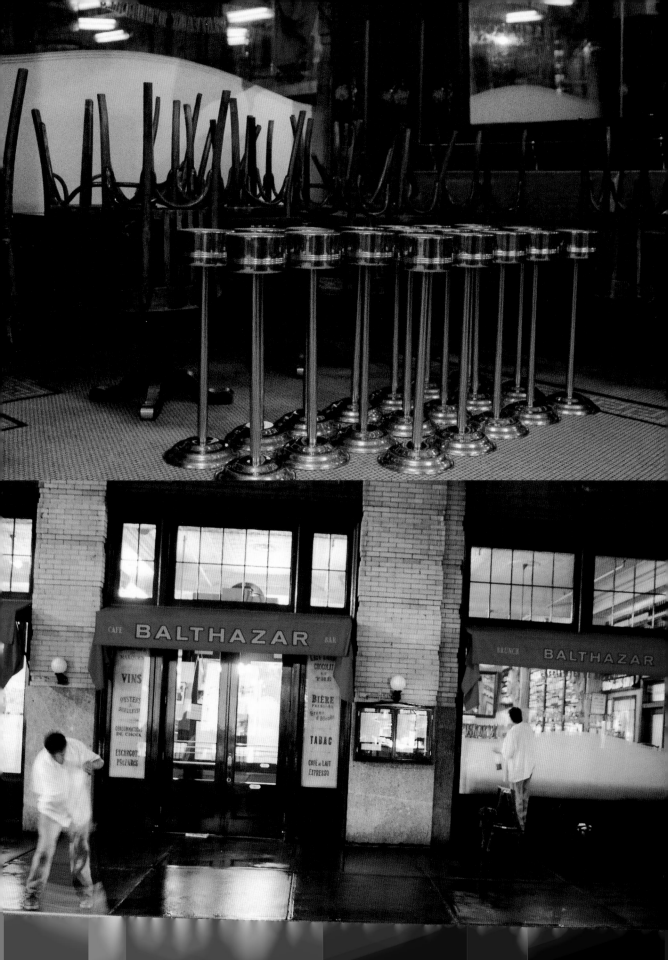

POUR FINIR

DESSERTS

CRÈME BRÛLÉE

The burnished sugar top of a crème brûlée should crack like thin ice over a custard that is neither cold nor hot, but cool. Shallow, 4-inch-wide ramekins offer a shard of caramelized sugar with every bite, the perfect ratio of torched top to creamy custard. This recipe works with the smaller but deeper ramekins as well.

SERVES 6

Preheat the oven to 300°F.

Combine the cream, ¼ cup of the granulated sugar, the vanilla bean and its seeds, and the cinnamon stick in a medium saucepan. Bring to a boil over a medium flame. Transfer the hot cream to a glass measuring cup.

Prepare an ice bath in a large mixing bowl. In a medium bowl (one that fits into the ice bath), lightly beat the egg yolks with a whisk. Slowly add the hot cream to the yolks in a steady stream, whisking all the while. Cool the bowl in the ice bath until the custard reaches room temperature, about 30 minutes.

Fill 6 ramekins nearly to the top with the custard, and place them in a large pan or casserole. Fill the pan with warm water until it reaches halfway up the sides of the ramekins. Cover with foil and bake for 45 minutes, or until the custard is set and firm when the ramekins are jiggled. Remove from the oven, let cool, and then refrigerate for at least 1 hour, or overnight.

Prior to serving, preheat the oven to 250°F. Combine the brown sugar with the remaining 2 tablespoons of granulated sugar. Dry the sugar mixture in the oven for 15 minutes and then mix in a food processor.

Evenly sprinkle 1 teaspoon of the sugar mixture over each custard, reaching to the rims. Brown the tops with a kitchen blowtorch, or slide under a broiler for 2 minutes until the sugar bubbles. Sprinkle another teaspoon of the sugar mixture over each custard and brown again. Serve immediately.

INGREDIENTS

2 cups heavy cream

¼ cup plus 2 tablespoons granulated sugar

1 vanilla bean, split with a knife, the small seeds scraped free from the bean

½ cinnamon stick

5 large egg yolks, lightly beaten

2 tablespoons light brown sugar

CHOCOLATE POT DE CRÈME

Named for the chubby porcelain pots that they're typically baked in, these chocolate custards are intensely flavored and smooth. Bake and serve them in the traditional lidded porcelains, ramekins, or even espresso cups. Experiment with combinations of bitter and milk chocolates for a varying depth of flavor—just be sure to use the best quality chocolate.

SERVES 6

Preheat the oven to 250°F.

In a medium saucepan, combine the cream, milk, sugar, and vanilla. Whisk to combine, and bring to a boil over a medium flame. Add the chopped chocolate and whisk until all the chocolate has melted. Remove from the heat.

In a medium bowl, lightly beat the egg yolks. Then, in a slow, steady stream, add in the chocolate-cream mixture, whisking until smooth.

Divide the mixture among 6 ramekins or small custard bowls (about 6 ounces each), and place them in a large casserole or high-sided baking dish. Make a bain-marie, or water bath, by pouring cold water into the casserole so that it comes halfway up the sides of the ramekins or custard bowls. Cover tightly with foil and bake on the center rack for 1 hour and 15 minutes. The custards should jiggle slightly in the center when finished. Let cool to room temperature and then refrigerate. Serve cool.

INGREDIENTS

1½ cups heavy cream
1 cup whole milk
½ cup sugar
1 teaspoon pure vanilla extract

8 ounces Valrhôna semisweet chocolate, coarsely chopped
6 large egg yolks

LEMON MILLE-FEUILLE

This dessert is a combination of a multilayered napoleon with a yellow frozen parfait that's topped by a granité. This delivers the powerful punch of citrus in varying textures and temperatures. You can make just the napoleon and, depending on your level of devotion, add on the other components.

SERVES 6

Bring about 2 inches of water to a simmer in a medium saucepan. (Choose a pan large enough to hold a medium heat-proof glass bowl above the simmering water.)

Combine the egg yolks, whole eggs, lemon juice, lemon zest, and ½ cup of the sugar in a medium heat-proof glass bowl and set over the simmering water. Whisk constantly until smooth, pale, and thick. Remove from the heat and whisk in the cubes of butter, one piece at a time, until the mixture has the consistency of stiff cake batter, about 15 minutes. Press plastic wrap against the surface of the lemon curd and refrigerate for at least 2 hours or overnight.

Lay a sheet of filo dough on a work surface (a parchment-lined cookie sheet is ideal). Using a pastry brush, thoroughly coat the entire surface of the filo with the melted clarified butter. Lay a second sheet of filo on top of that and, again, brush the sheet completely with a thin coating of clarified butter. Continue until all 7 sheets are stacked and buttered. Rest the filo in the refrigerator for 30 minutes.

Preheat the oven to 325°F.

With a sharp paring knife, trim the edges of the filo sheets so they're straight and uniform. With the help of a ruler, cut rectangles measuring 3½ by 1½ inches. There should be at least 18 pieces. Sprinkle 1 tablespoon of sugar on a parchment-lined baking sheet. Arrange the filo rectangles on the baking sheet, 3 rows down and 6 across, making sure that the edges of the rectangles touch one another. Sprinkle the remaining tablespoon of sugar over the filo and cover with another baking sheet, to ensure that the filo stays flat while it bakes. Bake for 20 minutes, or until golden brown. (Can be stored at room temperature in an airtight container.)

To assemble the napoleons, use a pastry bag with a #9 tip or a soup spoon. Lay 6 filo squares on a work surface. Pipe or spoon 2 dollops of the reserved lemon curd onto each rectangle and then gently press another rectangle of dough onto the lemon curd. Add a second layer of lemon curd on top of that and then top with the remaining 6 filo rectangles. Transfer to plates and serve with a slice of Frozen Lemon Parfait and a scoop of Lemon Granité alongside *(recipes follow)*.

INGREDIENTS

4 large egg yolks

4 large whole eggs

½ cup plus 2 tablespoons fresh lemon juice (from about 3 lemons), strained

Zest of 2 lemons, finely grated

½ cup plus 2 tablespoons sugar

2½ sticks unsalted butter, cut into ¼-inch squares, at room temperature

7 sheets filo dough

2 sticks clarified unsalted butter, melted *(see Note)*

CLARIFIED BUTTER

Clarified butter is butter from which the milk solids have been removed. It has a higher smoking point than regular butter and therefore doesn't burn as easily. To clarify butter, simply melt butter over a medium flame. Skim away any of the white milk solids that form along the edge of the pan. Use immediately or refrigerate for later use.

FROZEN LEMON PARFAIT

1 cup freshly squeezed lemon
  juice (from about 2 lemons)
1 cup sugar
2 cups heavy cream
4 large eggs, separated

Combine the lemon juice and ½ cup of the sugar in a small saucepan. Bring to a simmer, stir occasionally, and reduce to ½ cup of syrup, about 15 to 20 minutes. Strain.

Meanwhile, whip the heavy cream to soft peaks using the whip attachment on a standing mixer. Set aside in the refrigerator.

Combine the egg yolks and the syrup in the bowl of a standing mixer. Use the whip attachment and mix at medium speed for 5 minutes. Increase the speed to high and continue to beat for 10 minutes, until soft peaks form. Scrape the mixture into another bowl and wash and dry the metal mixing bowl and whip attachment. Pour the egg whites into the clean bowl and whisk on high speed until soft peaks form, about 2 minutes. Add the remaining ½ cup of sugar and mix to incorporate, about 10 seconds. Add the lemon–yolk mixture and whisk at low speed to combine. Remove the bowl from the mixer stand and fold in the reserved whipped cream.

Pour the mixture into a parchment-lined dish (13×8×2 inches). Press plastic wrap to the surface and then freeze.

LEMON GRANITÉ

1½ cups freshly squeezed lemon
   juice (from about 8 lemons)
 2 lemongrass stalks, smashed and
   cut into 1-inch pieces
 1 cup sugar

Combine all the ingredients in a medium saucepan and add 2 cups of water. Bring to a boil and cook for 10 minutes. Strain into a bowl or container and then transfer to the freezer. Hold at least overnight, and then scrape with an ice-cream scoop or large, sturdy metal spoon.

PINEAPPLE UPSIDE-DOWN CAKE

I n keeping with the atmosphere of the restaurant, the desserts at Balthazar tend to be unfussy and fun. This easy upside-down cake conveys that feeling quite effectively.

SERVES 6

Preheat the oven to 350°F.

Butter an 8- or 9-inch nonstick cake pan.

Sift the flour, baking soda, baking powder, and salt into a bowl. Set aside.

In a medium sauté pan, combine the brown sugar and the vanilla bean and seeds with 1 cup of water. Bring to a simmer. Add the pineapple and poach for 5 minutes. Remove the pineapple, raise the heat to high, and reduce the liquid to ¼ cup, about 10 minutes. Turn the heat off and stir in the rum. Set aside.

In the bowl of a standing mixer, combine the 6 remaining tablespoons of butter with the granulated sugar. With the paddle attachment, on medium speed, cream the butter and sugar until fluffy. Add the eggs one at a time and incorporate completely. Lower the speed and add the sifted ingredients. Mix on low for 10 seconds. Add the milk in increments and mix until smooth.

Arrange the pineapple slices in an overlapping circle on the bottom of the prepared cake pan and brush most of the rum-flavored syrup over them. Pour the batter over the slices to fill the cake pan halfway and bake for 30 minutes, rotating the pan after 15 minutes. Insert the blade of a knife into the center to test for doneness: It should come out clean. Let cool for 2 minutes before inverting onto a serving plate. Spoon the remaining glaze over the top.

INGREDIENTS

7 tablespoons unsalted butter, at room temperature	8 ⅛-inch slices fresh pineapple
1½ cups all-purpose flour	2 tablespoons coconut rum
¼ teaspoon baking soda	1 cup granulated sugar
½ teaspoon baking powder	2 large eggs
¼ teaspoon salt	¾ cup whole milk
¾ cup light brown sugar	
1 vanilla bean, split and scraped	

BANANA TARTE TATIN

WITH BANANA SABAYON

Efforts to take this off our regularly changing menu have met with great protest. As a result, this popular dessert has become a permanent fixture. Use 4-inch nonstick tart pans to make individual desserts.

SERVES 6

Combine the egg yolks, ¼ cup of the sugar, and the rum in a bowl that fits over a simmering saucepan of water. Set the bowl over the simmering water and whisk vigorously until the mixture becomes frothy and doubles in volume, about 5 to 8 minutes. Add the 2 mashed bananas and continue to whisk for another minute to incorporate. Cool the mixture and then transfer to the refrigerator to set, about an hour. Fold in the crème fraîche and the heavy cream and refrigerate the sabayon until needed.

Preheat the oven to 350°F.

Combine the remaining 1 cup of sugar with ¾ cup of water in a saucepan. Set over medium-high heat. Cook without stirring until the mixture begins to bubble and turns light amber. Swirl the pan and remove the pan from the heat. Spoon

2 tablespoons of caramel into each tart pan, tilting the pans to completely coat the bottom of each.

Roll out the puff pastry sheets to ¼-inch thick. Using a sharp knife, cut the pastry into 6 circles that are slightly larger than the top of the individual tart pans. Prick the dough several times with the tines of a fork. Arrange the banana slices in the tart pans, using 1 banana for each pan. Cover the banana layers with the precut rounds of puff pastry. (The tarts can be assembled to this point and then refrigerated for 1 day.)

Bake the tarts for 20 to 25 minutes, until the pastry is brown and puffy. Remove from the oven and invert onto plates using a spatula. Spoon the cool banana sabayon over the tarts and serve with vanilla ice cream alongside.

INGREDIENTS

4 large egg yolks	¼ cup crème fraîche
1¼ cups sugar	½ cup heavy cream
¼ cup dark rum	2 sheets of puff pastry
2 bananas, over-ripe and smoothly mashed, plus 6 firm bananas, thinly sliced	Vanilla ice cream, for serving

WARM CHOCOLATE CAKE

WITH MILK CHOCOLATE CRÈME ANGLAISE

A demanding public dictates that every restaurant must feature a signature chocolate cake. At Balthazar, the warm chocolate cake has a soft and stable center and is accompanied by a sweet chocolate crème anglaise.

SERVES 4

To make the crème anglaise: Melt the chocolate in a double boiler. Drizzle about ¼ cup of the melted chocolate into the lightly beaten egg yolks, whisking constantly. When completely blended, pour the tempered egg yolks back into the melted chocolate, again whisking the whole time. In a small saucepan, bring the cream, milk, and sugar to a simmer. Whisk ¼ cup of the warm cream into the melted chocolate in a slow stream. Then whisk the tempered chocolate mixture back into the saucepan. Set over a medium-low flame and bring to a simmer, whisking constantly, for 8 to 10 minutes, until it resembles thick pancake batter. Cool to room temperature and then cover with plastic wrap, pressing the wrap against the surface of the sauce to prevent a skin from forming. Refrigerate for up to 3 days but for at least 2 hours to chill before using.

To make the cake: Combine the whole eggs and the yolks with the sugar in the bowl of a standing mixer. Beat on high speed, using the paddle attachment, for 5 minutes, or until the mixture is pale and smooth.

Meanwhile, melt the chocolate and butter together in a double boiler. Slowly drizzle the melted chocolate into the egg–sugar mixture and continue beating until smooth. Reduce the speed of the mixer, add the flour, and mix rapidly to incorporate. Refrigerate for 1 hour or overnight.

Preheat the oven to 350°F.

Lightly grease six 4-inch ramekins with butter and dust with cocoa powder. Fill three-quarters full with the cake batter. Bake for 30 minutes, until the top of the cakes peak and crack but remain fudgy within.

Cool the cakes for about 3 to 5 minutes. Gently twist each in its ramekin and then turn the cake out into your palm. Plate and serve the cake warm with a few tablespoons of the chocolate crème anglaise spooned over, and vanilla ice cream alongside.

INGREDIENTS

FOR THE MILK CHOCOLATE CRÈME ANGLAISE

- 6 ounces milk chocolate, coarsely chopped
- 4 extra-large egg yolks, lightly beaten
- 1 cup heavy cream
- ½ cup whole milk
- ¼ cup granulated sugar

FOR THE CAKE

- 4 extra-large eggs
- 2 extra-large egg yolks
- 1 cup sugar
- 6 ounces dark chocolate, coarsely chopped
- 6 tablespoons unsalted butter, plus more for greasing ramekins
- ½ cup all-purpose flour, sifted
- ½ cup cocoa powder
- Vanilla ice cream, for serving

PROFITEROLES

At Balthazar, Profiteroles are served by a food runner who pours a warm chocolate sauce over the ice-cream-filled puffs, adding the finishing touch at the table. One runner began making a terrific show of all this, starting with a reserved drizzle, then gradually hoisting the little metal pitcher high above his head. Still pouring, he miraculously hits the ice cream target with no resulting splash. He began a trend among the food runners, all of whom now amaze and frighten the guests with their wild chocolate pouring.

SERVES 6

Preheat the oven to 350°F.

In a medium saucepan, combine the milk, butter, and salt with ½ cup of water and bring to a boil. Add the sifted flour and stir with a wooden spoon until thoroughly combined into a dough. Continue stirring over medium heat for about 3 minutes.

Transfer the dough into the bowl of a standing mixer. Stir at low speed for a few minutes to lower the temperature of the dough. Increase the speed to medium and then add the eggs, one at a time. Mix until a smooth, cool dough forms, about 4 minutes.

Fill a pastry bag, fitted with a #9 tip, with the dough, or use a soup spoon to form small puffs, about 2 inches in diameter,

on a parchment-lined baking sheet. Brush the puffs with the beaten egg yolk and transfer to the oven. Bake for 45 minutes, or until golden brown. Cool the puffs on a wire rack and then slice them, as if they were hamburger buns, with a serrated knife.

Make the chocolate sauce just before serving. Heat the heavy cream in a saucepan until it foams. Reduce the flame to low and add the chopped chocolate. Whisk until all the chocolate has melted and the sauce is smooth and shiny. Keep warm over a pan of simmering water.

Fill the puffs with a scant scoop of ice cream and serve on small plates or in shallow bowls. Pass a pitcher of warm chocolate sauce at the table.

FRENCH APPLE TART

Whether following a home-cooked meal or a fancy dinner, an apple tart is always appropriate and always appreciated. We serve ours warm with crème anglaise, but vanilla ice cream or crème fraîche would be fine alternatives.

SERVES 6

Preheat the oven to 350°F.

Peel 5 of the apples and cut them into ½-inch dice. Melt 4 tablespoons of the butter over medium heat. After the foam subsides, the butter will begin to turn brown. Add the diced apples and ½ cup of the sugar. Sauté for 3 to 4 minutes, until browned. Add the Calvados and let it bubble away, about 3 to 5 minutes, until only a syrupy glaze remains. Stir well with a wooden spoon, freeing any caramelized bits from the bottom of the pan. Set aside to cool.

Line a 10-inch false-bottom tart pan with the puff pastry and set the tart pan on a parchment-lined baking sheet. Prick the pastry several times with a fork and fill with the sautéed apples.

Peel and core the remaining 3 apples. Cut them in half and place them, flat side down, on a cutting board. Thinly slice and then arrange the slices over the sautéed apples, starting in the center, fanning them into concentric circles.

Melt the remaining 3 tablespoons of butter in a small saucepan. Brush the entire top of the tart with melted butter. Sprinkle with the remaining 1 tablespoon of sugar and bake for 18 to 20 minutes, until the top is golden brown. Cool for 10 minutes and serve with crème anglaise.

INGREDIENTS

8　Granny Smith or Golden Delicious apples

7　tablespoons unsalted butter

½　cup sugar plus 1 tablespoon for sprinkling

¼　cup Calvados

1　sheet of prepared puff pastry rolled to a 12-inch circle, ¼ inch thick

Crème Anglaise *(recipe follows)*, for serving

CRÈME ANGLAISE

2 cups whole milk
1 vanilla bean, split and scraped
4 extra-large egg yolks
½ cup sugar

Combine the milk and the split vanilla bean in a medium saucepan. Bring to a boil and remove from the heat. Pick out the vanilla bean and discard.

Combine the egg yolks and the sugar in a medium bowl. Whisk them together until the mixture is pale and smooth. Drizzle in a bit of the hot milk, whisking continuously, and completely incorporate before adding more milk in a slow stream. Continue until all the milk has been added.

Pour the mixture back into the saucepan and, over medium heat, continue to whisk for about 3 minutes, until the sauce has thickened. Use at room temperature or chilled.

PAVLOVA

As light and lithe as the ballerina for whom it was named, this dessert combines lush berries and sweet mascarpone, tucked into a pillow of meringue meant to resemble Anna Pavlova's tutu. This has a stylish, last-minute kind of elegance.

SERVES 6

INGREDIENTS

FOR THE MERINGUES
- 8 egg whites (about 6 ounces)
- 2 cups superfine sugar
- 1 teaspoon white wine vinegar
- 1 teaspoon vanilla extract

FOR THE BERRY COULIS
- 1 cup fresh strawberries, hulled
- 1 cup fresh raspberries
- 1 cup fresh blueberries
- 1 cup fresh blackberries
- ½ cup superfine sugar
- 1 tablespoon freshly squeezed lemon juice (from about ½ lemon)

FOR THE MASCARPONE CREAM
- 1 cup marscarpone cheese
- 1 cup plain yogurt
- ½ teaspoon lemon zest

For the meringues: Preheat the oven to 200°F. and line 2 baking sheets with parchment.

Combine the egg whites, sugar, vinegar, and vanilla extract in the bowl of an electric mixer fitted with a whisk attachment. Using a medium-high setting, beat the whites into stiff, shiny peaks.

Using a pastry bag with a #9 tip, pipe mounds of meringue that are about 3 inches in diameter and 3 inches high onto the baking sheets. (Alternatively, use a large serving spoon to form the meringues.) Bake until the meringues are ivory-colored and have a crisp exterior, about 3 hours. Cool to room temperature and store in an air-tight container for up to 3 days.

Prepare the berry coulis: Wash the berries in a colander and pick through, discard-ing any that seem overripe or damaged. Transfer half of the berries to a medium saucepan and add the sugar and lemon juice. Turn the flame to medium-low and stir until the berries start to break down. Continue to stir until a simmer is achieved, about 5 minutes. Press through a sieve and then cool. Refrigerate for up to 3 days.

To make the mascarpone cream, whisk the mascarpone, yogurt, and lemon zest together until thick and creamy. (Refrigerate for up to 3 days, and whisk again before serving.)

To serve the Pavlovas, tap the center of each meringue to form a nest. Warm the coulis in a saucepan, turn off the heat, and add the remaining whole berries. Spoon the mascarpone mixture into the center of each meringue, followed by several spoonfuls of the berry coulis.

BASIC

LES SAUCES ET
LES GARNITURES

RECIPES

CHICKEN STOCK

MAKES 2 QUARTS

Rinse the chicken bones and place them in a stockpot. Cover with 1 gallon of cold water and bring to a boil, skimming any foam that forms on the surface. Add the onions, celery, carrots, garlic, leek, thyme, bay leaves, parsley, and peppercorns.

Reduce to a simmer and cook for 2 hours, skimming as necessary. Remove from the heat, strain through a sieve, and cool. Store up to 5 days in the refrigerator or up to 1 month in the freezer.

INGREDIENTS

2 pounds chicken bones
2 onions, peeled and cut into 8 pieces each
2 celery stalks, cut into 1-inch pieces
2 carrots, cut into 1-inch pieces
4 garlic cloves, peeled

1 leek, green and white parts, cut into 1-inch pieces, well rinsed *(see page 144)*
4 sprigs of thyme
2 bay leaves
4 sprigs of flat-leaf parsley
1 teaspoon white peppercorns

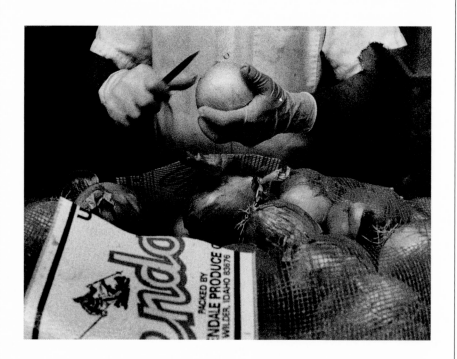

VEAL STOCK

Irreplaceable in the Balthazar kitchen, veal stock is made every other day, thirty gallons at a time. As the base for virtually every brown sauce and most stews, veal stock gets its considerable richness from the gelatinous shin bones of the veal. The long cooking time extracts every bit of this protein, which translates to an unbelievably silky stock, enriching everything in its path. Without a doubt, making veal stock at home is hard-core, the domain of the most dedicated cooks. But 8 hours of cooking time is rewarded with a stock that can transform a dish.

MAKES 1 QUART

Preheat the oven to 450°F.

Heat a dry roasting pan in the preheated oven for 15 minutes. Add the bones to the hot pan and roast until they are well browned, about 1½ hours. Use tongs to turn and rotate the bones throughout the cooking time.

When the bones are well browned, add the tomato paste and chopped vegetables. Toss to combine and continue roasting for an additional 30 minutes.

Transfer the contents of the roasting pan to a large stockpot and fill with water (about 8 quarts). Bring to a boil over high heat and skim off any foam that forms on the surface. Lower the heat to maintain a gentle simmer and cook for 5 to 6 hours, skimming fat from the surface every hour or so.

Strain the stock through a fine-mesh sieve. Cool and refrigerate for up to 3 days or freeze for up to 1 month.

INGREDIENTS

5 pounds veal bones
¼ cup tomato paste
1 yellow onion, roughly chopped
2 large carrots, roughly chopped
1 celery stalk, including green leaves
1 head of garlic, halved horizontally

ROAST CHICKEN JUS

Besides being an excellent gravy all on its own, jus—a reduction of roasted meat juices—is used as a base for many of the sauces we make. It has body without heaviness, and it tastes like the very essence of meat. It's easy to make in a restaurant where the surface area of our stockpots measures over 2 feet across, but it becomes trickier in the home kitchen. Most versions for this tend to simplify the recipe to the point where the finished product doesn't approach the deep and savory flavor that jus should possess. Here we scale things down from the professional-kitchen process, but it remains something of a production. Rather than use one pot and cook the chicken in four batches, giving the bottom of the pan ample time to burn and turn bitter, we work with two large pots, side by side. Is this worth the effort? For the dedicated cook, the answer is yes.

MAKES 2 CUPS

Using 2 large pots—say, a Dutch oven and a stockpot—heat 2 tablespoons of vegetable oil in each. When the oil begins to smoke, divide the chicken pieces between the pans, being sure not to crowd them: The surface of the pan should still be visible (if not, work in batches). Use tongs to turn the pieces over after about 5 minutes, and spoon off any excess rendered fat at this point. Reduce the flame to medium and continue to cook until the chicken pieces are a deep golden brown, about 10 minutes in all. Add 2 tablespoons of butter to each pan, stir to coat the chicken, and continue to cook for an additional 10 minutes, stirring occasionally. At this point the chicken should be a dark nut-brown. Reduce the heat to low, and divide the onion, garlic, and thyme between the pans. Cook for 5 minutes to brown the onion.

Turn the flame to high and add ½ cup of water to each pot. Reduce until the liquid is nearly dry, about 5 minutes. Add another ½ cup of water to each pot and, again, reduce until nearly dry. Add 3 cups of water to each pot, and bring each to a boil. At this point, and with confidence, transfer the contents of one pot into the other to combine, and simmer for 1 hour. Skim any fat that accumulates on the surface. Strain the liquid into a large saucepan and discard the solids. Over a medium flame, continue to reduce the liquid down to 2 cups, about 20 minutes. The jus can be held in the refrigerator for up to 3 days or frozen for up to 1 month.

INGREDIENTS

4 tablespoons vegetable oil

3 pounds chicken wings, cut into 2-inch pieces

4 tablespoons unsalted butter

1 onion, roughly chopped

4 garlic cloves, peeled and thinly sliced

4 sprigs of thyme

SWEET GARLIC JUS

To garnish the Mustard-Crusted Salmon (page 80), we add roasted garlic to the finished Roast Chicken Jus. Set the unpeeled cloves from 1 head of garlic on a large sheet of aluminum foil. Drizzle with olive oil and toss to coat. Crimp the foil closed to create a packet. Roast in a 400°F. oven for 45 minutes, until the garlic is tender. Squeeze the cloves from their skins to release the now soft and sweet garlic. Add 6 cloves of roasted garlic to simmering chicken jus and whisk to incorporate. Use the remaining roasted garlic in compound butters, mashed potatoes, polenta, or salad dressings. To store, squeeze the molten garlic into a bowl or jar, mash with a fork, and top with a small slick of olive oil. Keep covered, in the refrigerator, for up to 1 week.

COURT BOUILLON

Very old and very French, Court Bouillon is the classic poaching liquid for fish and shellfish. If using to cook shellfish for the Plateau des Fruits de Mer *(page 38)*, use the following recipe exactly. If using it for Escargots with Garlic Butter *(page 19)*, make the following adjustments: 2 celery stalks rather than 4; 1 bouquet garni rather than loose parsley, oregano, and bay leaves; and 1 quart of water rather than 2 gallons.

MAKES ABOUT 2 GALLONS

Place the carrot, celery, onion, and fennel in a stockpot. Add the wine, garlic, lemons, oregano, parsley, bay leaves, peppercorns, coriander seeds, salt, and 2 gallons of water.

Bring to a boil, then set to a simmer and cook for 25 minutes. Strain and discard the solids. Use immediately or refrigerate for 3 days, or freeze for later use.

INGREDIENTS

- 1 large carrot, roughly chopped
- 4 celery stalks, roughly chopped
- 1 large onion, diced large
- 1 fennel bulb, diced large
- 2 cups white wine
- 1 head of garlic, halved horizontally
- 4 lemons, halved
- 6 sprigs of fresh oregano
- 1 bunch of flat-leaf parsley, stems trimmed
- 3 bay leaves
- 1 tablespoon black peppercorns
- 1 tablespoon coriander seeds
- 1 tablespoon coarse salt

LEMON-TRUFFLE VINAIGRETTE

Besides making a great contribution to the success of the Balthazar Salad *(page 4),* this dressing would be a delicious addition to almost any salad, or just drizzled inside a sandwich.

MAKES 1 CUP

In a medium bowl combine the salt, pepper, and lemon juice. In a steady stream, whisk in the olive and truffle oils. Store covered in the refrigerator for up to 1 week. Whisk before using.

INGREDIENTS

½ teaspoon salt
¼ teaspoon freshly ground black pepper
Juice of 2 lemons (¼ cup)

¾ cup extra-virgin olive oil
¼ cup white truffle oil

SHERRY VINAIGRETTE

For salads, the oil and vinegar should be of the same high quality as the greens themselves. Use extra-virgin olive oil and top-quality sherry vinegar for this basic vinaigrette. Dress salads in a large bowl and then use spoons (or your clean hands) to transfer to a serving bowl, leaving excess dressing behind. Instead of olive oil, try hazelnut or walnut oil to add to your personal pantheon of salad dressings.

MAKES 1 CUP

In a mixing bowl, stir the salt and pepper into the vinegar. Whisk in the Dijon mustard and then add the oils in a steady stream, whisking constantly. Shake or whisk before use. Store covered in the refrigerator for up to 1 week.

INGREDIENTS

½ teaspoon salt
¼ teaspoon freshly ground
   black pepper
⅓ cup sherry vinegar

1 teaspoon Dijon mustard
⅓ cup extra-virgin olive
   oil
⅔ cup grapeseed oil

BALSAMIC VINAIGRETTE

A vinaigrette is 1 part vinegar and 3 parts oil whisked into an emulsion. Break out the best-quality extra-virgin olive oil for salad purposes, and experiment with all the wonderful vinegars, or swirl in a tablespoon of Tapenade *(page 238).*

MAKES 1 CUP

Using either a bowl with a whisk or a jar with a lid, add the olive oil to the vinegar and whisk or shake to combine. Add about ¼ teaspoon of sea salt and several gindings of black pepper. Keep at room temperature until needed or refrigerate for up to a week. Whisk immediately before using.

INGREDIENTS

- ¾ cup extra-virgin olive oil
- ¼ cup Modena balsamic vinegar

Sea salt and freshly ground black pepper to taste

TAPENADE

Whether spread on sandwiches or served alongside roasts, this classic Provençal condiment of pummeled olives is always handy and delicious. However, it's during cocktail hour, when served simply with croutons, that people seem to love it best. A food processor replaces the traditional mortar and pestle for faster results. Refrigerate for up to a week.

MAKES 1½ CUPS

Place all the ingredients except the olive oil in the work bowl of a food processor. Pulse to blend. Add the oil and pulse a few more times to form a cohesive but still coarse paste.

INGREDIENTS

½ pound black olives, pitted, drained of their liquid

4 anchovy fillets

2 tablespoons capers, drained

1 garlic clove, peeled

⅛ teaspoon cayenne pepper

¼ teaspoon grated orange zest

8 sprigs of thyme, leaves only

4 tablespoons olive oil

LEMON CONFIT

Bright and pleasant, these preserved lemons aren't the salted North African type, but more the sweet-and-sour kind. They enliven fish and most meats, and add an edge to salads.

Slice the lemons ¼ inch thick, discard the ends, and remove the seeds.

Bring a small saucepan of water to a boil and add the lemon slices. Boil them for 1 minute and then pour off the water. Add 1 cup of fresh water plus the sugar and vinegar and place over medium heat. Simmer for 20 minutes.

Cool to room temperature and then refrigerate the lemons in their cooking liquid for up to 2 weeks.

INGREDIENTS

4 lemons
½ cup sugar

½ cup white wine vinegar

RED ONION CONFIT

MAKES 2 CUPS

Combine the vinegar and sugar in a small saucepan. Add 1 cup of water and bring to a boil. Pour over the sliced onions in a medium bowl and cool to room temperature. Store the onions in the liquid until needed; they can be refrigerated, covered, for up to 1 week.

INGREDIENTS

1 cup red wine vinegar

⅓ cup sugar

2 red onions, thinly sliced

SWEET-AND-SOUR SHALLOTS

MAKES 1 CUP

Combine all the ingredients in a small saucepan and simmer for 45 minutes, or until the vinegars have been reduced almost entirely and all that remains is dark and slightly syrupy. Can be stored covered in the refrigerator for up to 2 weeks.

INGREDIENTS

7 shallots, peeled and diced very small

3 tablespoons granulated sugar

3 tablespoons light brown sugar

¾ cup sherry vinegar

¾ cup white wine vinegar

FENNEL CONFIT

Cooking anise-flavored fennel in olive oil leaves it soothingly soft in both texture and taste. The olive oil in which the fennel is cooked is delightfully infused with its flavor and can be used to dress salads or drizzle over fish.

MAKES 2 CUPS

Cut the fennel bulbs in half, remove the core, and cut into ¼-inch slices. Place all the ingredients in a medium saucepan and bring to a simmer over medium heat. Cook for 30 minutes. Cool the fennel to room temperature in the saucepan and then strain the oil into a bowl or bottle.

Store the infused oil in the refrigerator, covered, for another use. Store the fennel confit, covered, in the refrigerator for up to 2 weeks. Remove the star anise pods before serving.

INGREDIENTS

3	fennel bulbs, tough outer layer removed	½	teaspoon salt
3	cups extra-virgin olive oil	¼	teaspoon red pepper flakes
		4	star anise pods

TOMATO CONFIT

Even mid-winter tomatoes taste sweet and flavorful after a long slow roast in the oven. Oven-drying deepens their color and concentrates their character. The cooking time is long, but the effort and ingredient list are next to nothing.

MAKES 2 CUPS

Preheat the oven to 250°F.

Line a small baking sheet with aluminum foil. Spread the olive oil and garlic slices on the foil and add the halved tomatoes. With your fingers, toss the tomatoes in the oil to coat and then arrange the tomatoes, flesh side up, in 2 tightly formed rows. Sprinkle with the salt and pepper, place in the oven, and roast for 2 hours, turning and rotating the pan every half hour. When finished, the tomatoes will be soft, dry, and shrunken. Those tomatoes on the edge of the baking pan may finish cooking sooner than those in the center, so remove them to a plate to cool. Store the tomatoes in the refrigerator for 3 to 5 days, or submerge them in olive oil to refrigerate for a few weeks.

PEELING, SEEDING, AND DICING TOMATOES

Cut a small X at the bottom of each tomato with a paring knife. Bring a pot of water to a boil and set a large bowl of ice water near the stove. Drop the tomatoes in, a few at a time, for 20 seconds, then transfer to the ice water with a slotted spoon. When the tomatoes are cool enough to handle, pull the peels off starting at the X. (If there's resistance, slip them back into the boiling water for another few seconds.) Cut them in half through the stem and squeeze the seeds from each half. Remove the stem with a small V-shaped cut and dice the flesh.

3 tablespoons olive oil

1 garlic clove, peeled and thinly sliced

8 plum tomatoes, peeled and seeded *(see Note)*, halved

1 teaspoon salt

¼ teaspoon freshly ground black pepper

SAUCE AMÉRICAINE

Spoon this sauce over fish dishes like Cod with Lobster, Chickpeas, and Sauce Américaine *(page 72)* or Quenelles de Poisson *(page 18)*. This recipe is rated PG-13 due to its violent content.

MAKES 2 CUPS

2 live lobsters, about 1½ pounds each

6 tablespoons vegetable oil

½ medium yellow onion, thinly sliced

2 celery stalks, thinly sliced

2 medium carrots, thinly sliced

2 garlic cloves, thinly sliced

¼ cup brandy

6 plum tomatoes, roughly chopped

2 tablespoons tomato paste

¼ cup rice

½ teaspoon salt

Place a live lobster on a cutting board, claws toward you, tail away. Hold a heavy chef's knife with its sharp point in the center of the lobster's head, behind its eyes, at the ridge. With a swift motion, bring the point down into the head and then follow with the blade, putting your weight into the handle to kill the lobster (it will still be moving, though). Now pull the claws and the tail from the head. Split the head in two, rinse under cold water, and then chop each half into two pieces. Repeat with the other lobster.

Heat half the oil over a medium-high flame in a deep, straight-sided sauté pan for about 3 minutes. Add the tails and claws and cover with a tight-fitting lid. Cook the tails for 6 minutes and the claws for 8, flipping the pieces halfway through the cooking time. Remove from pan and set aside to cool.

Empty the oil out, scrape the bottom of the pan with the edge of a spatula to remove any burned bits, and then replenish the oil. Again over a medium-high flame, heat the oil until it's smoking, then add the head pieces. Cook uncovered for 5 minutes, until the shells are bright red.

Lower the flame to medium and add the onion, celery, carrots, and garlic. Cook until the vegetables begin to brown, stirring occasionally.

To remove the meat, use a sharp chef's knife to split the underside of the tail. Crack the tail toward you; the meat can then be easily pulled from the shell. For the claws, snap off the smaller, lower pincer and, with a chef's knife or cleaver, make a clean cut at the base of each claw, just above where it attaches to the knuckle. You can then pull the meat out in one piece. Chop the meat into 2-inch chunks and refrigerate until needed. Reserve the shells.

When the vegetables are lightly caramelized, add the brandy, tomatoes, tomato paste, and reserved shells. Bring to a simmer and cook for 30 minutes. Add the rice and cook for an additional 20 minutes, until the rice is tender.

Use tongs to remove the lobster shells and then pour the contents of the pan into the blender and purée until smooth. Strain the sauce and season with the salt. Use immediately or refrigerate to be reheated on the stove or in the microwave.

SAUCE BORDELAISE

The famous sauce of Bordeaux, enriched with Veal Stock *(page 231)* and the local wine, is a key component in the recipe for Oeufs en Meurette *(page 34)*. Use it as a gravy for almost any beef dish.

MAKES 1 CUP

Season the beef cubes with the salt and pepper. In a Dutch oven or heavy-bottomed skillet, heat the oil over a medium-high flame. When it begins to smoke, add the meat (work in batches if necessary) and brown well on all sides, 3 to 5 minutes per side. When all the beef is well browned, add the shallots and cook for about 5 minutes, stirring frequently, until the shallots brown. Add the head of garlic and the bouquet garni, and follow with the red wine. Raise the flame to high to bring to a boil and use a wooden spoon to free any caramelized bits from the pan. When the liquid has reduced by three quarters, about 12 to 15 minutes, and what remains is thick and dark, add the Veal Stock. Bring to a boil, and use a spoon or ladle to skim the surface of any fat or impurities that accumulate. Lower the flame to medium and simmer for 35 to 40 minutes, until the sauce is thick and brown, with an appetizing consistency (it will coat the back of a wooden spoon). Strain and discard solids. Store covered in the refrigerator for 1 week, or freeze.

INGREDIENTS

- 1 pound inexpensive stew meat or beef shank meat, cut into 1-inch cubes
- ½ teaspoon salt
- ¼ teaspoon freshly ground black pepper
- 3 tablespoons vegetable oil
- 6 shallots, sliced (about ½ cup)
- 1 head of garlic, halved horizontally
- 1 bouquet garni *(see page 31)*
- 3 cups dry red wine
- 3 cups Veal Stock *(page 231)*

ROASTED BELL PEPPERS

We roast peppers using two different methods: over a flame and in the oven. Flame-roasting is convenient when roasting just a few peppers, because it's as simple as setting the pepper over a burner and allowing direct contact with the flame. While the whole pepper sits on the flame, the skin turns black, blisters, and is then easily rubbed off by hand. The pepper is then cored and sliced.

Oven-roasting, however, produces a more mellow flavor, with a softer, moist flesh, preferable in fresh salads or on sandwiches. There's also the added benefit of being able to roast a whole pan's worth at once. Choose whatever method is most appealing according to need and convenience.

MAKES 6 PEPPERS

Preheat the oven to 400°F. Line a baking sheet with aluminum foil. Toss the peppers with the olive oil. Lay the peppers, skin side up, on the lined baking sheet. Sprinkle with the salt. Bake for 30 to 45 minutes, until the skin blisters and blackens. Remove from the oven, put the peppers in a bowl, and cover tightly with plastic wrap. The accumulation of heat will cause the skins to bubble and separate from the flesh. When they're cool enough to handle, the skins can be pulled off easily.

Use immediately or store in the refrigerator, submerged in olive oil and covered.

INGREDIENTS

6 bell peppers, any color, cored and stemmed, cut into wide strips

½ cup olive oil
2 teaspoons salt

MAYONNAISE

Mayonnaise is the very first thing students learn to make in cooking school. Once homemade mayonnaise is mastered, there seems little reason to go back to the jarred kind. Starting with a slow trickle of oil is the crucial technique. We use a few drops of Tabasco and Worcestershire to add a little heat.

MAKES 1 CUP

Put all the ingredients except for the oils in the bowl of a food processor. Blend for 30 seconds. With the blade still spinning, drizzle the grapeseed oil in a very slow stream, followed by the olive oil. This should take about 2 minutes. As the mayonnaise forms, the noise from the food processor will become louder, making a slapping sound, as it does with cake batter. Process until the mayonnaise is thick, with a creamy body. Refrigerate, covered, for up to 1 week.

INGREDIENTS

- 2 large egg yolks
- 2 teaspoons Dijon mustard
- 2 teaspoons fresh-squeezed lemon juice
- 1 teaspoon sherry vinegar
- ½ teaspoon Worcestershire sauce
- ½ teaspoon Tabasco sauce
- ½ teaspoon salt
- ½ cup grapeseed oil
- ½ cup olive oil

TARTARE MAYONNAISE

To serve with Steak Tartare (page 26), add the following ingredients to the prepared Mayonnaise, and whisk to smoothly combine.

- ½ cup ketchup
- 3 tablespoons Dijon mustard
- 1 teaspoon Tabasco sauce
- 1 teaspoon Worcestershire sauce
- ½ teaspoon salt

AÏOLI

This golden mayonnaise of Provence receives its color from saffron and its spiciness from Tabasco and garlic. Quick and easy to make, aïoli is mandatory with Bouillabaisse *(page 46)*.

(page 46)

MAKES 1 CUP

Combine the saffron and the hot water and steep for about 5 minutes. Combine the egg yolks, garlic, Tabasco, salt, and lemon juice in the bowl of a food processor. Add the steeped saffron and water and blend for 30 seconds. With the blades still spinning, add the olive oil in a slow, steady stream until an emulsion forms. Refrigerate, covered, for up to 1 week.

INGREDIENTS

- $\frac{1}{2}$ teaspoon saffron threads
- 2 tablespoons hot water
- 2 large egg yolks
- 2 garlic cloves, peeled and minced
- $\frac{1}{2}$ teaspoon Tabasco sauce
- $\frac{1}{2}$ teaspoon salt
- 1 tablespoon fresh lemon juice (from about $\frac{1}{2}$ lemon)
- 1 cup olive oil

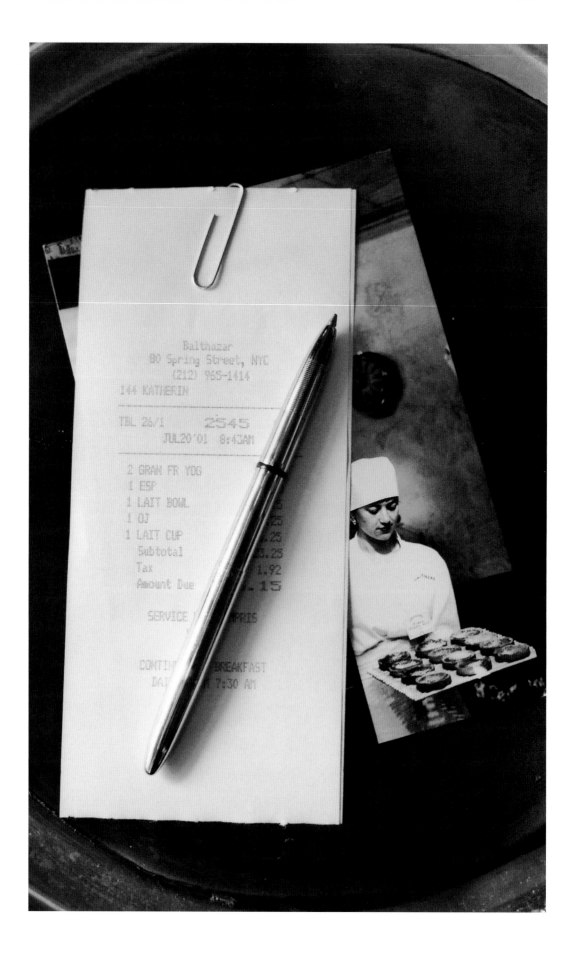

❧

— A C K N O W L E D G M E N T S —

I'd like to thank my mother, Joyce Woodroof. —K.M.

Restaurants (and books) are built on hard work and sacrifice. I'd like to thank all our staff and coworkers, past and present, and Keith McNally, Lee Hanson, my family, my mother, Diane O'Young, sister, Samira Nasr, and wife, Donna "She Wolf." —R.N.

Thanks to my mother, Karen Coyle, who got me hooked on the energy and chaos of a restaurant kitchen when I was just eight years old. Although she worked tirelessly to support us, she always had time to help me achieve my goals. The deepest gratitude to my greatest teacher, Daniel Boulud, in whose kitchen I met life-altering food and friends. A bow to Sottha Khunn, my Jedi master. To Riad Nasr, my pal on and off the ice. To Keith McNally, for giving us this great opportunity along with the support and trust that made us grow as a team, and whose ideas I can't wait to steal. To my wonderful, foxy wife, Kathryn, who, since the day Balthazar opened, has always been understanding about the long hours and late-night hockey games: You are a constant source of comfort and rejuvenation and forever my class wit. And lastly, my beautiful little Maya, who brought a twinkle to my eye and joy to my heart. —L.H.

— CONVERSION CHART —

EQUIVALENT IMPERIAL AND METRIC MEASUREMENTS

American cooks use standard containers, the 8-ounce cup and a tablespoon that takes exactly 16 level fillings to fill that cup level. Measuring by cup makes it very difficult to give weight equivalents, as a cup of densely packed butter will weigh considerably more than a cup of flour. The easiest way therefore to deal with cup measurements in recipes is to take the amount by volume rather than by weight. Thus the equation reads:

1 cup = 240 ml = 8 fl. oz.   ½ cup = 120 ml = 4 fl. oz.

It is possible to buy a set of American cup measures in major stores around the world.

In the States, butter is often measured in sticks. One stick is the equivalent of 8 tablespoons. One tablespoon of butter is therefore the equivalent to ½ ounce/15 grams.

LIQUID MEASURES

Fluid Ounces	U.S.	Imperial	Milliliters
	1 teaspoon	1 teaspoon	5
¼	2 teaspoons	1 dessertspoon	10
½	1 tablespoon	1 tablespoon	14
1	2 tablespoons	2 tablespoons	28
2	¼ cup	4 tablespoons	56
4	½ cup		120
5		¼ pint or 1 gill	140
6	¾ cup		170
8	1 cup		240
9			250 (¼ liter)
10	1¼ cups	½ pint	280
12	1½ cups		340
15		¾ pint	420
16	2 cups		450
18	2¼ cups		500 (½ liter)
20	2½ cups	1 pint	560
24	3 cups		675
25		1¼ pints	700
27	3½ cups		750
30	3¾ cups	1½ pints	840
32	4 cups or 1 quart		900
35		1¾ pints	980
36	4½ cups		1000 (1 liter)
40	5 cups	2 pints or 1 quart	1120

SOLID MEASURES

U.S. and Imperial Measures		Metric Measures	
Ounces	Pounds	Grams	Kilos
1		28	
2		56	
3½		100	
4	¼	112	
5		140	
6		168	
8	½	225	
9		250	¼
12	¾	340	
16	1	450	
18		500	½
20	1¼	560	
24	1½	675	
27		750	¾
28	1¾	780	
32	2	900	
36	2¼	1000	1
40	2½	1100	
48	3	1350	
54		1500	1½

OVEN TEMPERATURE EQUIVALENTS

Fahrenheit	Celsius	Gas Mark	Description
225	110	¼	Cool
250	130	½	
275	140	1	Very Slow
300	150	2	
325	170	3	Slow
350	180	4	Moderate
375	190	5	
400	200	6	Moderately Hot
425	220	7	Fairly Hot
450	230	8	Hot
475	240	9	Very Hot
500	250	10	Extremely Hot

Any broiling recipes can be used with the grill of the oven, but beware of high-temperature grills.

EQUIVALENTS FOR INGREDIENTS

all-purpose flour—plain flour
baking sheet—oven tray
buttermilk—ordinary milk
cheesecloth—muslin
coarse salt—kitchen salt
cornstarch—cornflour

eggplant—aubergine
granulated sugar—caster sugar
half and half—12% fat milk
heavy cream—double cream
light cream—single cream
parchment paper—greaseproof paper

plastic wrap—cling film
scallion—spring onion
shortening—white fat
unbleached flour—strong, white flour
zest—rind
zucchini—courgettes or marrow